the savoury
gluten-free baker

the savoury gluten-free baker

60 delicious recipes for the gluten intolerant

Hannah Miles

photography by William Reavell

RYLAND PETERS & SMALL
LONDON • NEW YORK

Dedication
In loving memory of Kathie Taylor, who tasted many of the recipes in this book.

Senior Designer Iona Hoyle
Editor Rebecca Woods
Head of Production Patricia Harrington
Art Director Leslie Harrington
Editorial Director Julia Charles

Prop Stylist Lisa Harrison
Food Stylists Bridget Sargeson and Jack Sargeson
Indexer Hilary Bird

First published in 2013 by Ryland Peters & Small
20–21 Jockey's Fields, London WC1R 4BW
and
Ryland Peters & Small Inc.
519 Broadway, 5th Floor
New York, NY 10012

www.rylandpeters.com

10 9 8 7 6 5 4 3 2 1

Text © Hannah Miles 2013
Design and photographs © Ryland Peters
& Small 2013

UK ISBN: 978-1-84975-465-1
US ISBN: 978-1-84975-429-3

A CIP record for this book is available from the British Library.

US Library of Congress cataloguing-in-publication data has been applied for.

Printed and bound in China

Coeliac UK is a leading charity working for people living with coeliac disease and dermatitis herpetiformis. Visit them at www.coeliac.org.uk or call the Helpline on 0845 305 2060 for information and support. In the US visit www.celiac.org or www.celiac.com for information, advice and support.

contents

Introduction

The positive response to my first gluten-free baking book is something that I am immensely proud of, and I was delighted to be asked to write a companion book. Developing these recipes in the knowledge that they will make a difference to people who can't eat gluten and wheat was a project I relished and enjoyed immensely, even if at times a few of the recipes were challenging! The end result is a collection of easy-to-make-at-home savoury recipes for all those favourite dishes that those on a gluten-free diet miss the most.

Being diagnosed as having a gluten allergy or wheat intolerance can be extremely daunting as wheat and gluten are so commonly used in modern day cooking. All those quick lunches and suppers, such as sandwiches and pasta, appear initially problematic and the alternatives offered in supermarkets are not always as tasty as their non gluten-free counterparts. Although I am able to eat gluten myself, one of my closest friends, Lucy, is allergic to wheat and I know first hand from her just how difficult coming to terms with a gluten-free diet can be. In this book I have sought to include all those recipes that Lucy says she misses the most – toad in the hole, crumpets, naan breads, sausage rolls, tarts and quiches – all of which are easy to make at home yourself with gluten-free flours that are readily available in supermarkets or online.

Before writing my first gluten-free baking book, I read a lot of books on gluten-free cooking to try and help Lucy find some new recipes for her change in diet. Most required a lot of flour combining and a lengthy list of non-store cupboard ingredients. There was no clear explanation of which flour to use when and in what quantities. All in all, it was very intimidating, even for someone who bakes as much as I do. What I wanted was some good basic recipes that used ingredients that I was familiar with, gluten-free plain and self-raising flours, polenta and such like. Ready-combined flours seemed the simplest solution and avoided the need for combining many different types of gluten-free flour – such as tapioca, potato and rice – as they have already been combined by the manufacturers in what I imagine must be the best possible combination following rigorous testing. Using these ready-blended flours lets you bake as you would with regular flour and achieve excellent results. Keep two or three bags in the kitchen store cupboard and you can bake perfect gluten-free breads, pastry and treats whenever needed. It is then just a question of understanding the characteristics of the particular gluten-free flours you are using, and adding other ingredients to provide the extra moisture needed and plenty of flavour. Not all gluten-free flours are the same, so some will need more liquid than others

One thing I have noticed about most people who are not able to eat gluten is that they don't want to stand out as different – they just want to be served something 'normal' and not be made to feel like they are causing inconvenience. The aim of this book is therefore simple: to make things that taste so good that you would never know they were gluten-free and that can therefore be served to everyone. These recipes are designed to be eaten by the whole family, even those who can eat gluten, so that you can avoid the need to bake two different recipes for each occasion.

This book provides delicious alternatives to those favourite savoury baking recipes that people suffering from coeliac disease, gluten intolerance or wheat allergy miss the most – breads, tarts, quiches, pies – dishes which are perfect for simple suppers, picnics or elegant dinners. With a little know-how and some simple ingredients, this book will enable you to create delicious dishes at home.

My hope is that this book will give you all the tools and the confidence you need to rustle up delicious tarts, pies and breads for yourself and others. Mixing bowls at the ready – let's get baking!

What is Coeliac Disease?

Coeliac disease is an auto-immune disease which affects the intestines, leading to poor absorption of gluten. Symptoms of coeliac disease can leave those affected feeling very unwell and lacking in energy, as well as having an upset stomach and other ailments. There is currently no cure for the condition but it can be managed very well by changing to a diet which omits gluten products. It is important that medical advice is taken by anyone who feels they might be experiencing a sensitivity to gluten, to ascertain whether they are a coeliac or are experiencing an allergic reaction to gluten and/or wheat. Each person's symptoms are unique – some people will be able to eat some ingredients that are problematic for others. Testing is available and it is important to take steps to understand what is safe for you to eat. For my friend Lucy, this was a steep learning curve, but within a few months she knew which brands of chocolate, poppadoms and stock cubes didn't contain gluten and were safe for her to enjoy. Sometimes coeliac disease is also coupled with other allergies and you may find that some other products, which are gluten-free, also make you unwell. A common example of this is an intolerance to dairy, although this is usually transient. With time and experience you will have a clear understanding of your own limitations. Keeping a food diary can be of great assistance at the outset to enable you to monitor and identify any problem foods.

Gluten is present in varying levels in wheat, barley and rye cereals and also sometimes in oats, although this is thought to be most likely caused by cross-contamination with other cereals. Some people sensitive to gluten can eat oats and as these are a good staple ingredient in baking, some of the recipes in this book use them, but always make sure you buy brands labelled 'gluten-free' to be safe. You should always check, however, whether the person you are baking for is intolerant to oats.

Managing a Gluten-free Diet

Whilst it is easy to avoid products that obviously contain wheat and gluten – such as bread, cakes or pasta – there are a variety of products that contain traces of gluten, some of which are not obvious. It is not always easy to avoid such pitfalls and it is, therefore, essential to carefully check the ingredients list on product packaging or refer to the manufacturer to ensure that a product is gluten-free.

Some brands of a type of product may be gluten-free whereas other brands may not – very careful reading of ingredients labels is always essential. Nowadays many products are clearly labelled as 'gluten-free', which makes life much easier.

All forms of wheat, barley, rye and spelt must be avoided. This means that regular flours and breads are out, as well as wheat-based products, such as beer and pasta. However, there are now a good range of gluten-free breads, pasta and beer available in most supermarkets.

Gluten is also commonly used by food manufacturers in a wide variety of food preparation processes and can be found in ready-meals and other processed foods. A small trace of wheat used as a thickener in a sauce may make you really unwell, but checking the labelling will help you to spot unsafe ingredients. Many varieties of products which used to contain gluten, such as baking powder, are now regularly made with rice flour making them gluten free. Always check the labels carefully though.

Shredded suet is used in several pastry recipes in this book and it is important to ensure that it is coated in gluten-free flour rather than wheat flour. Products that are coated in breadcrumbs are also not suitable for people with gluten intolerance.

You need to be extra vigilant at all stages of cooking. It is so easy to take a packet from the kitchen cupboard and add to a recipe without checking whether the item contains gluten – I have found myself doing this on occasion and have just stopped myself in time. With time and practice you will become familiar with which ingredients are safe and which are not. The best advice is just to take a bit of time before you start cooking. Assemble all of your ingredients and check that they are all safe to use before starting to bake.

Some of the less obvious products that may contain gluten include:

Anti-caking agents – these are used to prevent clumping and sticking together of ingredients during food production and can contain traces of wheat. Anti-caking agents are commonly found in products such as suet but also in icing/confectioners' sugar and dried fruits.

Yeast – some dried yeasts contain wheat as a bulking agent. For safe gluten-free baking, use either fresh yeast or a gluten-free dried yeast, both of which are stocked by most supermarkets and health food shops.

Baking powder – some baking powders contain wheat. Many manufacturers are now using rice flour in place of wheat flour and so gluten-free baking powder is now more commonly available in supermarkets.

Malt products – malted drinks should all be avoided as they are wheat based, but malt extract can usually be tolerated in small amounts, for example in breakfast cereals. Malt vinegar is suitable as the protein is removed in the fermentation process and the traces left are tolerated by the vast majority of coeliacs.

Soy sauce and Worcestershire sauce – these also contain gluten so look out for gluten-free brands. Tamari soy sauce is often gluten free.

Processed meat products – products such as sausages, sausagemeat, salamis and pâtés can contain traces of wheat, so always read the labels carefully. In recipes which call for sausagemeat, such as the sausage rolls on pages 80 and 84, I find it best to buy gluten-free sausages and remove the meat from the skins. Most packs of sausagemeat that I have found contain gluten as the meat is bulked with breadcrumbs.

Sauces, gravy powders, stocks (cubes and liquid)

and powdered spices – these products can sometimes be bulked out with wheat products so, again, always check the labels carefully.

Instant coffees – some contain wheat as a bulking agent. Fresh ground coffee, which can be used to make espresso or filter coffee in a machine can be used instead as these generally do not contain any gluten.

Sour cream – some processes for making sour cream use wheat so it is important to use a brand that is 'pure' and gluten free. Checking the manufacturers' website will assist with this.

The above list is not exhaustive but it should give you a good idea of just how rigorous you have to be with product checking when you are cooking for someone with a gluten intolerance.

Gluten-free Baking

The key to successful gluten-free baking is to understand the ingredients and their properties. Gluten gives elasticity to the doughs from which breads and pastries are made. Gluten-free substitutes lack this elasticity and need to be handled slightly differently. The good news is that as the doughs are not elastic, they generally require no, or minimal, kneading, sparing your arm muscles somewhat! Generally speaking, gluten-free doughs and mixes require a lot more liquid than wheat-based recipes and if insufficient liquid is added, the end result can have a powdery texture and crumble when you cut into it. Adding natural yogurt, buttermilk or sour cream can help with this, as will adding cheese or cream cheese and egg yolks to pastry to act as a binding agent.

Pastry can be very crumbly without the elasticity of gluten and must be very carefully worked. Rather than rolling the pastry out into large sheets that are likely to crumble when lifted, the best method for making a pastry case is to gently press small pieces of the pastry dough into the tin/pan until it is lined entirely with a thin layer of pastry. If the pastry does crack, do not worry as you can easily patch the cracks with off cuts of pastry and once baked, these will not show at all. Gluten-free suet crust pastry and choux pastry both work really well and give such a good result that I do not think anyone would know they are gluten free. I have used a suet crust on pies and for the Beef Wellingtons on page 112 as the suet binds the pastry together and does not crack very much on baking (a common problem with gluten-free pastry), ensuring that your pie or wellington filling is perfectly encased. If you can't find shredded suet, you can substitute vegetable shortening. In order that it doesn't make the pastry too sticky, the chilled shortening should be coarsely grated and dusted lightly with gluten-free flour. Freeze the flour-coated shortening for about 60 minutes and use straight from the freezer in place of the suet.

Some gluten-free flours can have a slightly bitter taste that can spoil the flavour of baked goods. The best way to mask this is to make sure that each recipe is packed full of flavour.

The Gluten-free Baking Pantry

For successful baking you need to equip yourself with a few basic ingredients. Once you have developed confidence from following these recipes, you can then experiment with other recipes. Below is a list of essential ingredients you will need for baking the recipes from this book.

Gluten-free blended flours – there is now a wide variety of gluten-free flours available in supermarkets and wholefood stores and these are the easiest flours to start with. They are ready mixed and are specifically designed to give the best results. In the UK four types are available – plain flour which is ideal for pastry and biscuits/cookies, self-raising flour for cakes and some breads, strong white bread flour for breads and some pastries, and strong brown bread flour for bread. In the US all-purpose flour is available but I've yet to find a self-raising/rising one so have tested the recipes in this book with Bob's Red Mill gluten-free all-purpose baking flour, adding gluten-free baking powder and xanthan gum, which gives a very good result. If you are not able to obtain gluten-free bread flour, you can use plain/all-purpose flour

and add 1½ teaspoons of xanthan gum to every 125 g/1 cup of flour. Whilst the results are, of course, best with bread flour (as it has been specifically designed to make great bread), this conversion will enable you to still enjoy the recipes. Whilst you can combine your own mixes of rice, potato and cornflour/cornstarch, I personally find it more convenient to use these ready-mixed flours.

Gram flour – this is made from ground chickpeas and is often used in Indian cookery. It can be used to make pakora and bhajis as well as various Indian flatbreads. Most poppadoms are made with gram flour, but it is important to check that it has not been combined with wheat flour. Italian farina di ceci is a similar product and can be substituted.

Cornflour/cornstarch – this is made from finely ground grains of corn. It is an excellent thickener and can be used in sauces.

Polenta/cornmeal – this is a useful staple of gluten-free baking. Coarse grains can be cooked in water to a thick paste and added to savoury muffins and breads to give a lovely golden colour, moist texture and rich flavour. Fine cornmeal is more like flour in texture and can be used in breads and muffins. Several of the recipes

11

in this book use yellow fine-grain cornflour/cornstarch, which has a slightly nutty texture and is great as a topping on the Courgette Bread on page 44 and for coating the Gnudi on page 131.

Quinoa flour – this flour is made from ground quinoa grains which are gluten free, nutritious and have a great texture. It is particularly good for making pasta. It has quite a strong, slightly medicinal smell and I therefore always use it combined with other flours.

Ondhwa flour – this is an Indian flour made from ground rice and lentils and is available in Indian supermarkets and online. If you are not able to find this flour, there are several recipes on line for how to make the flour at home yourself.

Oat Flour – this is made from finely ground oats. As stated on page 9, some oats contain traces of gluten so it is important to ensure that the oat flour you use is gluten free and that the person you are cooking for can eat oats. Oat flour is available from health food shops and online.

Oats – not all people who are intolerant to gluten are able to eat oats. The protein in oats is similar to gluten and so can also be an issue for some coeliacs, although it may cause different symptoms. If in doubt, do not use them. However, there are many people who are intolerant to gluten who are able to eat oats, but make sure you choose brands labelled gluten-free to be sure that they are free from cross-contamination with other cereals.

Almond meal and ground almonds – almond meal is a coarse ground flour which contains the skin of the whole almonds. It is therefore darker in texture than ground almonds. Ground almonds are useful in gluten-free baking (predominantly sweet recipes) as they give cakes lots of moisture and do not have a strong flavour so can carry other flavours well. You can make your own ground almonds or almond meal by blitzing whole or skinned almonds in a food processor. When buying ready-ground almonds, check the ingredients as some cheap varieties include breadcrumbs as a bulking agent (and therefore gluten).

Gluten-free baking powder – this is an essential raising agent, which is used to make cakes and breads rise during baking.

Xanthan gum – this is used in gluten-free baking to bind, thicken and stabilize ingredients and is ideal for use in doughs, pastry and breads. It's made by fermenting corn sugar with a microbial bacteria and is used extensively in the food industry.

Flavouring agents – flavourings are ideal for masking the sometimes mildly unpleasant 'flavour' of gluten-free flours. In this book I have used truffle oil, dried mushrooms, Parmesan cheese, black pepper and mustard. Always check the labelling to ensure that flavourings are gluten free.

Dairy ingredients – these are essential in gluten-free baking given the crumbly nature of gluten-free doughs and mixes. The recipes in this book use buttermilk, plain yogurt and sour cream. Again, it is essential to check the product labels as some creams may contain traces of gluten from the manufacturing process. If you prefer, you can make your own sour cream by adding the juice of a lemon to 300 ml/1¼ cups double/heavy cream. If you do not have the liquid ingredient called for in the recipe, you can easily substitute – for example if you do not have buttermilk, mix together half milk and half plain yogurt to the same quantity of buttermilk. The results will be equally delicious.

Eggs – eggs do not contain gluten and are used in many of the recipes in this book.

Butter and fats – some margarines may contain gluten, so it is best to use good-quality unsalted butter in all recipes to remain gluten-free.

Alcohols – this can be a slightly confusing area for those who are gluten-intolerant. Beer is made with hops and so must be avoided. Some brands of whisky (and cream-based whisky liqueurs) may contain gluten from the caramel colouring which is added, although pure whisky does not contain gluten. Before using any alcohol, check with the manufacturer to ascertain whether it is gluten-free.

Avoiding Contamination

One key requirement of successful gluten-free baking is to avoid cross-contamination. If you have a member of the family who is intolerant to gluten, the best solution is to remove all products containing gluten from the house. Whilst this is the most effective way to avoid the risk of cross contamination, I recognize that this is not always practical. Where total removal is not possible, the best advice is to keep gluten-free products in sealed containers in a separate place away from products containing gluten. Label everything clearly so that there can be no confusion as to what is gluten-free.

If you have been baking with regular flour, small particles will have been released into the air during cooking, which can land on cooking equipment, surfaces and even kitchen towels and leave traces of gluten. It is therefore very important to wipe down all equipment, surfaces and utensils thoroughly and use clean cloths and aprons. It takes a surprisingly small amount of exposure to gluten to make someone ill.

Cross-contamination is also possible through using kitchen appliances and equipment, such as toasters, baking sheets and wire cooling racks. Silicon sleeves (Toastabags) can be used to shield toasters from gluten contamination or, if possible, have a separate toaster and other similar appliances just for gluten-free products. Also consider investing in some silicon mats that you can set aside just for gluten-free baking. It is also important to avoid putting knives and spoons that have been exposed to gluten into butters, spreads and jams/jellies as these can also cause contamination. If it is practical, have separate tubs and jars clearly labelled as 'gluten-free'. Where possible, store these away from products that may contain traces of gluten.

Where to Go for Advice

If you believe that you may have a gluten intolerance or coeliac disease, it is essential to seek professional medical advice. Once you have been diagnosed with either, there are many sources of information available to you. The Coeliac Societies in the UK and USA are able to provide a large amount of advice and support (see page 4). Local support groups can also offer guidance on managing day-to-day life without gluten. In addition, there are a wide variety of books on this subject as well as some fantastic online communities offering a wealth of information. Particularly useful are the forums where coeliacs can communicate with each other and share advice on all aspects of living and enjoying a gluten-free lifestyle.

muffins & scones

These muffins encapsulate the main elements of a classic English fried breakfast, with bacon, tomatoes and even a whole egg on top. They are best served straight from the oven while still warm. Use high-sided muffin cases, which can hold a whole egg, and don't overfill with the muffin mixture, otherwise your eggs will spill over.

breakfast muffins

Preheat the oven to 180°C (350°F) Gas 4.

Reserve 6 small strips of bacon to decorate the muffins and blitz the remaining bacon to fine crumbs in a food processor.

In a large mixing bowl, whisk together the butter, sugar, large egg and the bacon crumbs. Add the flour (plus baking powder and xanthan gum, if using), almonds, cornmeal and crème fraîche and whisk well so that everything is incorporated. Season with salt and pepper.

Place a large spoonful of the batter into each of the muffin cases and top with 2 tomato halves, then cover the tomatoes with another spoonful of batter. Carefully crack one of the small eggs into a bowl, then pour it onto the top of one of the muffins, taking care that it doesn't spill over the edge of the case (hold back a little of the egg white if the case is close to overflowing). Repeat with the remaining 5 small eggs and muffins. Sprinkle a little black pepper over each egg and lay one of the reserved bacon strips on top of each muffin. Bake the muffins in the preheated oven for 15–20 minutes and serve straight away.

30 g/1 oz. crispy cooked smoked bacon rashers/slices
60 g/4 tablespoons butter, softened
1 tablespoon caster/granulated sugar
6 small eggs, plus one large egg
45 g gluten-free self-raising flour OR ⅓ cup gluten-free all-purpose flour plus ½ teaspoon baking powder and ¼ teaspoon xanthan gum
15 g/2 tablespoons ground almonds
15 g/2 tablespoons fine cornmeal
1 tablespoon crème fraîche or sour cream
6 cherry vine tomatoes, halved
sea salt and ground black pepper

a 6-hole large muffin pan lined with 6 high-sided muffin cases

Makes 6

The humble crumpet – so comforting spread with butter – is one of the things my friend Lucy misses most on her gluten-free diet. We have tried several store-bought versions but none of them are as nice as their wheat counterparts. This is our recipe, which is, in Lucy's view, a huge improvement on store-bought gluten-free crumpets.

crumpets

1 tablespoon caster/granulated sugar

1 tablespoon fast-action dried yeast

400 ml/1⅔ cups warm milk

300 ml/1¼ cups warm water

300 g/2⅓ cups gluten-free strong white bread flour

150 g/1 cup plus 2 tablespoons gluten-free plain/all-purpose flour

1 teaspoon baking powder

½ teaspoon bicarbonate of soda/baking soda

½ teaspoon salt

1 teaspoon vanilla extract

butter, melted, for greasing

4 x 9-cm/3½-inch chefs' or crumpet rings

Makes 10–12

Put the sugar and yeast in a jug/pitcher with the warm milk and water. Leave for about 10 minutes in a warm place until a thick foam forms on top of the liquid.

Sift the flours, baking powder and bicarbonate of soda/baking soda into a large mixing bowl and whisk in the salt and vanilla along with the yeast mixture. Cover the bowl with clingfilm/plastic wrap and leave for 45 minutes in a warm place until the mixture has doubled in size.

Grease the chef's rings lightly with butter. Grease a frying pan or griddle with a little butter and set it over medium heat. Place the chefs' rings in the pan and pour a small ladleful of the crumpet batter into each ring. Cook for about 10 minutes until holes form on top of the crumpet, then remove the rings using oven gloves. Turn the crumpets over and cook for a further 5–10 minutes until the crumpet is golden brown and there is no scrunching noise when you press your finger down on top of the crumpet. When cooked, remove the crumpets from the pan or griddle and repeat the process until all the batter is used.

The crumpets are best served warm so eat them straight away, or if you are serving later that day, toast them to reheat before serving. They freeze well and can be toasted from frozen.

19

There are few finer breakfasts than a toasted muffin topped with hollandaise, poached eggs and ham, in the classic Eggs Benedict.

english muffins with eggs benedict

Put the warm milk, yeast and sugar in a jug/pitcher and leave in a warm place for about 10 minutes until a thick foam has formed on top of the liquid.

Sift the flour, baking powder and xanthan gum into a large mixing bowl. Add the salt, egg, yogurt, melted butter and mix well with a wooden spoon until everything is incorporated and you have a soft dough. Divide the dough into 6 portions.

Dust a clean surface with yellow cornflour/cornmeal and roll each dough portion into a ball. Flatten the balls into patties, turning with your hands so that the muffin is flat on the top and bottom and has straight sides about 3 cm/1 inch high. Sprinkle the muffins with polenta and pat down so that it sticks to the dough, then place them on a flour-dusted baking sheet and leave, uncovered, in a warm place for 45–60 minutes.

When the muffins have risen, heat a griddle pan or frying pan over a high heat. Grease the pan with a little butter. Add the muffins to the pan, then turn down the heat. Cook the muffins for about 8–10 minutes on one side and then turn over and cook for a further 7–10 minutes on the other side so that the muffins are golden brown on both sides and spring back to your touch when you press them and do not feel doughy. (You may find it easier to cook the muffins in batches.)

To make the hollandaise, simmer the vinegar and the juice of 1 lemon in a saucepan with the bay leaf and some black pepper for about 2 minutes until the liquid has reduced by half. Remove the bay leaf and season with salt and pepper, then pour the liquid into a food processor with the egg and egg yolks and blend together. Melt the butter in a saucepan, then, with the blade still running and the butter warm, pour it into the egg mixture in a thin drizzle. Whisk until the mixture becomes slightly thick. Taste for seasoning, adding a little further lemon juice and salt and pepper if needed.

When you are ready to serve, bring a saucepan of water to the boil, add the vinegar and season. Turn down the heat so that the water is just simmering. Break the eggs, one at a time, into a cup and carefully tip into the water. Poach the eggs for 2–3 minutes, then remove from the water with a slotted spoon. The eggs should still have a golden runny yolk, so take care not to overcook them.

While the eggs are cooking, cut the muffins in half and toast until lightly golden brown. Top each pair of muffin halves with a slice of ham and a poached egg, spoon over some of the warm hollandaise, season and serve straight away.

150 ml/⅔ cup warm milk

1 tablespoon fast-action dried yeast

1 tablespoon caster/granulated sugar

300 g/2⅓ cups gluten-free strong white bread flour

1 teaspoon baking powder

1 teaspoon xanthan gum

1 teaspoon salt

1 egg, beaten

80 ml/⅓ cup set plain yogurt

60 g/4 tablespoons butter, melted and cooled

yellow cornflour/fine cornmeal and polenta grains, for dusting

For the hollandaise

1 tablespoon white wine vinegar

freshly squeezed juice of 1–1½ lemons

1 bay leaf

1 whole egg, plus 2 egg yolks

190 g/1 stick plus 5 tablespoons butter

sea salt and ground black pepper

To serve

1 teaspoon white wine vinegar

6 eggs

6 slices of thick cut ham

Makes 6

These muffins are bursting with tomato and make a delicious savoury snack, or are delicious served on the side of a bowl of soup or a fresh salad. The added delights of feta and fresh basil will transport you to the Mediterranean and sunny days.

tomato, basil & feta muffins

350 g gluten-free self-raising flour plus 1 teaspoon baking powder OR 2¾ cups gluten-free all-purpose flour plus 4 teaspoons baking powder and 2 teaspoons xanthan gum

1 teaspoon bicarbonate of soda/baking soda

250 ml/1 cup milk

250 ml/1 cup plain yogurt

2 eggs

100 g/6½ tablespoons butter, melted and cooled

2 tablespoons tomato purée/paste

160 g/¾ cup (drained weight) sundried tomatoes preserved in oil, chopped, plus one tablespoon of the oil

200 g/7 oz. feta cheese, chopped into small pieces

3 tablespoons chopped fresh basil leaves

sea salt and ground black pepper

2 muffin pans lined with 16 muffin cases

Makes 16

Preheat the oven to 180°C (350°F) Gas 4.

Sift the flour, baking powder (plus xanthan gum, if using) and bicarbonate of soda/baking soda into a large mixing bowl.

In a separate bowl, whisk together the milk, yogurt, eggs, melted butter and tomato purée/paste, then add this to the flour mixture. Whisk everything together well and season with salt and pepper. Mix the tomatoes and feta cheese into the mixture, along with the tomato oil and the chopped basil.

Divide the mixture between the muffin cases, making sure that some of the pieces of cheese and sundried tomato sit on the top of each muffin. Bake the muffins in the preheated oven for 20–30 minutes until golden brown. Serve warm or cold.

The muffins will keep for up to 2 days in an airtight container, but can be frozen and then reheated to serve.

These lovely muffins are an ideal accompaniment to soup. Packed with both puréed corn and whole kernels, they are deliciously moist and full of flavour.

sweetcorn muffins

Preheat the oven to 180°C (350°F) Gas 4.

Sift the flour, baking powder (plus xanthan gum, if using) and bicarbonate of soda/baking soda into a mixing bowl and stir in the cornmeal.

Blitz half of the sweetcorn/corn kernels to a smooth purée in a food processor, and add it to the flour mixture.

In a separate bowl, whisk together the milk, eggs, crème fraîche and melted butter, then add to the flour mixture. Whisk everything together well, adding the sugar and seasoning with salt and pepper. Stir through most of the remaining whole sweetcorn/corn kernels, reserving a few kernels to sprinkle on top of the muffins.

Divide the mixture between the muffin cases and top with the remaining corn. Bake in the preheated oven for 25–30 minutes until golden brown and the muffins spring back to your touch. Serve warm or cold.

The muffins will keep for up to 2 days in an airtight container but can be frozen and then reheated to serve.

200 g gluten-free self-raising flour plus 1 teaspoon baking powder OR 1⅔ cups gluten-free all-purpose flour plus 2¾ teaspoons baking powder and 1¼ teaspoons xanthan gum

1 teaspoon bicarbonate of soda/baking soda

50 g/⅓ cup fine cornmeal

330 g/1⅔ cups sweetcorn/corn kernels

150 ml/⅔ cup milk

2 eggs

4 tablespoons/¼ cup crème fraîche or sour cream

100 g/6½ tablespoons butter, melted and cooled

1 tablespoon caster/granulated sugar

sea salt and ground black pepper

2 muffin pans lined with
16 muffin cases

Makes 16

These dense muffins are kept really soft and moist with the addition of mashed potato. Sage has quite a strong flavour and if you are not keen on it you can substitute 2 tablespoons of finely chopped chives instead, adding them to the potato with the melted butter.

sage & potato muffins

400 g/14 oz. potatoes, peeled and chopped

165 g/1 stick plus 3 tablespoons butter

15 small sage leaves, cut into thin strips

1 tablespoon caster/granulated sugar

2 eggs

115 g gluten-free self-raising flour plus 2 teaspoons baking powder OR scant 1 cup gluten-free all-purpose flour plus 3 teaspoons baking powder and ¾ teaspoon xanthan gum

2 tablespoons crème fraîche or sour cream

a 12-hole muffin pan lined with muffin cases

Makes 12

Boil the potatoes in salted water for about 20 minutes until soft.

Preheat the oven to 180°C (350°F) Gas 4.

Heat 50 g/3½ tablespoons of the butter in a frying pan and fry the sage leaves until crispy. Pour the melted sage butter over the cooked potatoes and mash with a potato masher until smooth, then leave to cool.

Whisk together the remaining butter and the sugar in a large mixing bowl. Add the eggs, flour, baking powder (plus xanthan gum, if using), crème fraîche and cooled potato and whisk until the batter is smooth. Spoon the mixture into the muffin cases and bake in the preheated oven for 35–45 minutes until the muffins are golden brown. These muffins are best served warm.

These muffins are quick and simple to prepare and are deliciously light and tasty. Needing only a few ingredients, they are a great standby recipe. To make them dairy- and gluten-free, omit the cheese and replace with some corn kernels instead.

cheese & onion soufflé muffins

Preheat the oven to 180°C (350°F) Gas 4.

In a frying pan, cook the onion in the oil until softened and lightly golden brown, then leave to cool.

In a mixing bowl, stir together the egg yolks, cooked onion and grated cheese, and season with salt and pepper.

Put the egg whites in a separate bowl and whisk them to stiff peaks.

Gently fold the egg whites into the cheese mixture with a spatula until the cheese and onions are evenly distributed through the egg. Spoon the mixture into the holes of the muffin pan and bake in the preheated oven for 20–25 minutes until the soufflés have risen and are golden brown. Remove the muffins from the pan while still warm. These muffins are best served straight away.

1 onion, finely chopped

1 tablespoon oil

5 eggs, separated

125 g/1¼ cups grated red Leicester or mature/sharp Cheddar cheese

sea salt and ground black pepper

a 12-hole muffin pan, well greased

Makes 12

These loaf cakes are tangy from the creamy taleggio cheese, moist from the grated courgette/zucchini and have a great crunchy hazelnut topping. Whenever I make them, they disappear straight away!

taleggio & hazelnut loaf cakes

115 g/1 stick butter, softened

1 tablespoon caster/granulated sugar

2 eggs

115 g gluten-free self-raising flour OR scant 1 cup gluten-free all-purpose flour plus 1 teaspoon baking powder and ¾ teaspoon xanthan gum

200 g/7 oz. taleggio cheese, rind removed and chopped into small pieces

1 tablespoon crème fraîche or sour cream

1 courgette/zucchini, grated

2 tablespoons roasted and chopped hazelnuts

sea salt and ground black pepper

8 mini loaf cases

Makes 8

Preheat the oven to 180°C (350°F) Gas 4.

In a large mixing bowl, whisk together the butter, sugar, eggs and flour (plus baking powder and xanthan gum, if using). Add the taleggio pieces, crème fraîche and grated courgette/zucchini to the mixture, season well with salt and pepper, and fold everything together.

Spoon the batter into the loaf cases and sprinkle the tops with chopped hazelnuts. Bake in the preheated oven for 25–30 minutes until the cakes are golden brown and spring back to your touch. Leave to cool before serving.

The cakes will keep for up to 2 days in an airtight container.

31

A cheese scone, served warm from the oven and spread with butter, is one of life's pleasures. These scones contain four different types of cheese – salty Parmesan, creamy mascarpone, tangy Cheddar and golden red Leicester.

four cheese scones

Preheat the oven to 180°C (350°F) Gas 4.

Sift the flour and baking powder (plus xanthan gum, if using) into a large mixing bowl, add the ground almonds and butter and rub in the butter with your fingertips until the mixture resembles fine breadcrumbs. Mix in the mascarpone cheese, then fold in the Parmesan and two thirds of the Cheddar and red Leicester cheeses, reserving a third of each to top the scones. Gradually add the milk and bring together into a soft dough, adding a little more milk if needed.

On a flour-dusted surface, roll out the dough to about 2.5 cm/1 inch thick and stamp out the scones using the pastry cutter, re-rolling the trimmings as necessary. (You should only re-roll the dough once as it will become crumbly with the extra flour and difficult to roll.) Lay the scones on the prepared baking sheet, spacing them well apart. Use a pastry brush to brush the tops with a little extra milk, sprinkle over the remaining cheese and top with a little cracked black pepper. Bake in the preheated oven for 20–25 minutes until the tops are golden and the scones sound hollow when you tap them. Serve warm or cold.

The scones do not keep well and so are best eaten on the day they are made or can be frozen and reheated to serve.

350 g gluten-free self-raising flour plus 2 teaspoons baking powder OR 2¾ cups gluten-free all-purpose flour plus 5 teaspoons baking powder and 2 teaspoons xanthan gum, plus extra flour for dusting

100 g/⅔ cup ground almonds

115 g/1 stick butter, chilled and cubed

70 g/⅓ cup mascarpone cheese

20 g/⅓ cup grated Parmesan cheese

120 g/1 generous cup grated Cheddar cheese

120 g/1 generous cup grated red Leicester cheese*

200–250 ml/¾–1 cup milk, plus extra to glaze

freshly ground black pepper

a 7.5-cm/3-inch round fluted pastry cutter

a baking sheet, greased and lined with non-stick baking paper

Makes 10

*If you can't find red Leicester, you can substitute any other hard cheese, or use double the quantity of Cheddar.

I love sweet dainty Madeleine cakes and these pumpkin versions are no less delicious. They make a tasty accompaniment to soups and stews but can be eaten on their own as a snack. It is important to chill the Madeleine batter before cooking to get the best results. Make these in a mini Madeleine pan for bite-size canapés, if you prefer.

pumpkin madeleines with sage

100 g/6½ tablespoons butter, plus extra for greasing

12 sage leaves

2 eggs

20 g/1½ tablespoons caster/granulated sugar

100 g/scant ½ cup pumpkin purée

70 g gluten-free self-raising flour OR ½ cup plus 1 tablespoon gluten-free all-purpose flour, plus ¾ teaspoon baking powder and ½ teaspoon xanthan gum

50 g/⅓ cup ground almonds

sea salt and ground black pepper

a 12-hole large Madeleine pan, greased with butter

a piping bag fitted with a large round nozzle/tip

Makes 12

Set a frying pan over a gentle heat, add the butter and heat until foamy (make sure you cook the butter over a gentle heat to ensure that it does not brown too much). Add the sage leaves and cook for a few minutes until the leaves are slightly crispy, then remove the leaves with a slotted spoon and reserve the butter. Place one sage leaf into each hole of the greased Madeline pan, securing in place in the centre with a little butter.

For the Madeleine mixture, whisk together the eggs and sugar in a large mixing bowl until the mixture is thick and creamy. Add the pumpkin purée, flour (plus baking powder and xanthan gum, if using) and almonds and whisk in. Add the cooled, melted sage-infused butter from the frying pan and mix together well. Season with salt and pepper, then spoon the batter into the piping bag and chill in the refrigerator for 1 hour.

Preheat the oven to 180°C (350°F) Gas 4.

Pipe the mixture into the holes of the Madeleine pan, then bake in the preheated oven for 15–20 minutes, until golden brown and the Madeleines spring back to your touch.

I prefer to eat these warm and they are best eaten on the day they are made.

The spicy oil from the chorizo imparts its flavour into these delicious scones as they bake. They are great served warm spread with paprika butter. Whipped butters are a real treat and although they take a few minutes to make, the result is definitely worthwhile.

chorizo & manchego scones

Preheat the oven to 180°C (350°F) Gas 4.

Cut the chorizo into small pieces and dry fry in a frying pan until the chorizo releases its oil and the edges start to turn crispy. Leave to cool.

Sift the flour and baking powder (plus xanthan gum, if using) into a large mixing bowl, add the ground almonds and butter and rub in the butter with your fingertips until the mixture resembles fine breadcrumbs. Add the cubes of Manchego to the flour mixture, along with the chorizo and any oil from the frying pan and season with a little salt and pepper. Gradually add the milk and bring together into a soft dough, adding a little more milk if needed.

On a flour-dusted surface, roll out the dough to about 2.5 cm/1 inch thick and stamp out the scones using the pastry cutter, re-rolling the trimmings as necessary. (You should only re-roll the dough once as it will become crumbly with the extra flour and difficult to roll.) Lay the scones on the prepared baking sheet, spacing them well apart. Use a pastry brush to brush the tops with a little extra milk, sprinkle with a little paprika and sugar. Bake the scones in the preheated oven for 20–25 minutes until the tops are golden and the scones sound hollow when you tap them.

Make the paprika butter just before serving as it will lose its whipped texture if refrigerated. Whip the butter in a stand mixer or with an electric hand whisk for a few minutes with the salt and paprika until it is light and creamy. Serve the scones warm with the whipped butter.

The scones do not keep well and so are best eaten on the day they are made or can be frozen and reheated to serve.

For the scones

100 g/3½ oz. gluten-free spicy chorizo sausage

350 g gluten-free self-raising flour plus 2 teaspoons baking powder OR 2¾ cups gluten-free all-purpose flour plus 5 teaspoons baking powder and 2 teaspoons xanthan gum, plus extra flour for dusting

100 g/⅔ cup ground almonds

115 g/1 stick butter

100 g/3½ oz. Manchego cheese, cut into small cubes

200–250 ml/¾–1 cup milk, plus extra to glaze

paprika, to sprinkle

caster/granulated sugar, to sprinkle

sea salt and ground black pepper

For the paprika butter

115 g/1 stick butter, softened

1 teaspoon sea salt flakes

1 teaspoon hot smoked paprika

a baking sheet, greased and lined with non-stick baking paper

an 8-cm/3½-inch triangle pastry cutter

Makes 10

breads & doughs

Brioche does take a long time to make but one slice of this buttery bread and you will realise that it is definitely worth the effort. The dough will be quite sticky before the first proving, but don't worry as it will become more manageable and easy to handle after proving.

brioche

Put the warm water in a jug/pitcher with the yeast and 1 tablespoon of the sugar and leave in a warm place for about 10 minutes until a thick foam has formed on top of the liquid.

Sift the flour and xanthan gum into the bowl of the stand mixer and add the remaining sugar. Pour in the yeast liquid and mix with a dough hook for 2–3 minutes. With the mixer running, beat in the eggs one at a time until you have a smooth dough. Once all the eggs are added, mix the dough for a further 3 or so minutes until it is smooth and silky.

Add the butter, cube by cube, to the dough whilst still mixing, until all the butter is incorporated and the dough is glossy and comes away from the sides of the bowl. The dough will be quite sticky. Cover the bowl with lightly greased clingfilm/plastic wrap and leave to prove in a warm place for about 3 hours until the dough has doubled in size. Knock back the dough on a flour-dusted surface and knead again with your hands, dusting liberally with flour.

Divide the dough in half, shape into two balls and place one in each of the prepared brioche pans. Whisk together the egg and sugar for the glaze and brush over the dough with a pastry brush (you may not need it all). Cover each loaf lightly with a layer of clingfilm/plastic wrap and leave in a warm place for 1–2 hours until the loaves have doubled in size again.

Preheat the oven to 180°C (350°F) Gas 4 and bake the brioche for 25–30 minutes until they are golden brown and sound hollow when you tap them.

The brioche is best eaten warm from the oven spread with butter and preserves.

For the brioche

60 ml/¼ cup warm water

7 g/1 envelope fast-action dried yeast

70 g/⅓ cup caster/granulated sugar

500 g/4 cups gluten-free strong white bread flour, plus extra for dusting

1 teaspoon xanthan gum

7 eggs

375 g/3 sticks plus 2 tablespoons butter, slightly softened and cubed

For the glaze

1 egg

2 tablespoons caster/granulated sugar

a stand mixer fitted with dough hook

2 brioche pans, about 16 cm/ 6½ inches diameter, greased

Makes 2 loaves

This is a delicious autumnal focaccia bread, topped with crunchy nuts and plump, juicy raisins that have been soaked in sherry. It makes a great accompaniment to all sorts of soups and salads, or enjoyed on its own as a snack. It is best served warm on the day it is made.

walnut & raisin focaccia

100 g/⅔ cup raisins

125 ml/½ cup sherry

7 g/1 envelope fast-action dried yeast

1 tablespoon caster/granulated sugar

80 ml/⅓ cup warm water

450 g/3½ cups gluten-free strong white bread flour

250 ml/1 cup warm milk

2 eggs, beaten

1 teaspoon balsamic vinegar

1 teaspoon salt

100 g/⅔ cup walnut halves

a few sprigs of fresh rosemary

olive oil, for drizzling

sea salt flakes

a 33 x 23-cm/13 x 9-inch shallow-sided baking pan, greased with olive oil

Makes 1 large loaf

Begin by soaking the raisins in the sherry for about 3 hours until the fruit has plumped up.

Put the yeast, sugar and warm water in a jug/pitcher and leave in a warm place for about 10 minutes until a thick foam forms on top of the liquid.

Sift the flour into a large mixing bowl and add the yeast mixture, warm milk, eggs, vinegar and salt and whisk together until everything is incorporated. Spoon the mixture into the baking pan, cover with a damp tea/dish towel and leave in a warm place for 1 hour until the dough has doubled in size and risen.

Preheat the oven to 190°C (375°F) Gas 5.

Drain the raisins and sprinkle them over the dough, along with the walnuts. Poke small sprigs of rosemary into the dough at regular intervals. Drizzle the loaf generously with olive oil and sprinkle with sea salt. Bake in the preheated oven for 35–40 minutes until the bread springs back to the touch and has a crusty top. Serve warm or cold.

The focaccia is best eaten on the day it is made.

This tasty bread is perfect with soups and cheese. It has a pretty courgette/zucchini and a cornmeal topping, which gives the top of the loaf a nice crunchy coating. If you prefer blue cheese, you can substitute this for the Cheddar for a more piquant flavour.

courgette bread

Preheat the oven to 180°C (350°F) Gas 4.

Sift the flour, baking powder (plus xanthan gum, if using) and cornmeal into a large mixing bowl. Add the beaten eggs to the flour along with the melted butter and milk, then fold in the grated cheese.

Grate one of the courgettes/zucchini and add it to the mixture, folding everything together well. Season with salt and pepper, then spoon the mixture into the prepared cake pan.

Finely slice the remaining courgette/zucchini using a mandolin or a sharp knife. Lay the courgette/zucchini slices in lines on top of the mixture in the pan and sprinkle over a little freshly ground black pepper. Dust the courgette/zucchini slices with cornmeal, then lightly dab the olive oil over the top of the loaf using a pastry brush.

Bake the bread in the preheated oven for 40–50 minutes, until the top is golden and the loaf springs back to your touch. Leave the loaf to cool in the pan for 5 minutes, then turn out onto a wire rack to cool completely.

200 g gluten-free self-raising flour plus 3 teaspoons baking powder OR 1⅔ cups gluten-free all-purpose flour plus 4¾ teaspoons baking powder and 1¼ teaspoons xanthan gum

100 g/¾ cup fine cornmeal, plus extra for dusting

3 eggs, beaten

60 g/4 tablespoons butter, melted and cooled

300 ml/1¼ cups milk

150 g/5½ oz. applewood smoked Cheddar, grated

2 courgettes/zucchini (about 350 g/12 oz.), ends trimmed

olive oil for brushing

sea salt and ground black pepper

a mandolin (optional)

a 24-cm/10-inch loose-based square cake pan, greased and lined with non-stick baking paper

Makes 1 loaf

44

Soda bread is traditionally from Ireland and is very quick and easy to prepare. It contains no yeast as the recipe uses bicarbonate of soda/ baking soda to make it rise. It is great to serve with soups and casseroles. Cutting the cross on top of the loaf is important as it allows it to cook all the way through.

soda bread

350 g/2¾ cups gluten-free strong brown bread flour, plus extra for dusting

200 g/1½ cups oat flour*

1 teaspoon bicarbonate of soda/baking soda

1 teaspoon salt

500 g/2 cups buttermilk

80 ml/⅓ cup milk

a baking sheet, greased

Makes 1 loaf

*Oat flour is available in health food shops and online, but if you cannot find it substitute gluten-free plain/all-purpose flour instead.

Preheat the oven to 180°C (350°F) Gas 4.

Put the bread and oat flours in a large mixing bowl and add the bicarbonate of soda/baking soda and the salt. Add the buttermilk and milk and mix to form a soft dough. If it is too sticky, add a little more flour but don't overwork the dough – as there is no yeast, you need to keep the mixture as light as possible.

Form the dough into a round mound, about 4 cm/ 1½ inches high and 20 cm/8 inches in diameter. Cut a cross on the top of the loaf with a sharp knife and dust the top with a little extra flour. Put the loaf on the prepared baking sheet and bake in the preheated oven for 45–55 minutes until the bread is crusty on top and makes a hollow sound when tapped.

The bread is best eaten on the day you make it, but can be reheated in the oven the following day.

47

With a sumptuous filling of mozzarella and roasted vegetables, a large wedge of this picnic loaf is a meal in itself – perfect fast food on the go! The actual amount of filling needed will depend on the size of the loaf you use, so the given quantities are guidelines only.

rustic picnic loaf

Preheat the oven to 180°C (350°F) Gas 4.

Put the tomatoes and courgette/zucchini in a roasting pan and drizzle with the olive oil and balsamic vinegar. Sprinkle with the sugar and season with salt and pepper. Bake the vegetables in the preheated oven for 25–30 minutes until they are very soft. Set aside to cool in the pan, reserving any juices as they will be added to the dressing.

Bake the bread according to the packet instructions, then leave to cool. Once cool, slice open the baguette or slice the top off the loaf and set aside. Gently pull out the inside of the loaf so that you have a hollow crust with a thin layer of bread inside, making sure that you do not make any holes in the crust.

Put the roasted tomatoes and courgette/zucchini in a bowl with the spring onion/scallion, mint and basil. Whisk together the oil and lime juice and the roasting juices from the pan, season with salt and pepper and pour over the vegetable and herb mixture. Gently fold together so that the vegetables are well coated with the dressing.

To fill your loaf, begin by lining the bottom and sides with some spinach leaves as these will prevent the filling from making the bread soggy. Cover the base with a layer of red peppers, then spoon in some of the tomato mixture, pressing down with the back of a spoon. Top with mozzarella slices and sprinkle over half of the olives. Repeat the layers until the loaf is very fully and firmly packed, then finish with a layer of spinach leaves. Close the baguette, or cover the loaf with the bread lid, and wrap the bread tightly in clingfilm/plastic wrap. Chill for 2 hours then unwrap and cut into slices to serve. (Transport the loaf wrapped in the clingfilm/plastic wrap and cut it on your picnic for best results.)

Alternatively, if you are staying at home, this sandwich is also delicious warm – remove the clingfilm/plastic wrap and bake at 180°C (350°F) Gas 4 for about 15–20 minutes, until the cheese has melted.

For the roasted vegetables
150 g/5½ oz. vine cherry
   tomatoes
1 courgette/zucchini, ends
   removed and cut into batons
2 tablespoons olive oil
1 tablespoon balsamic vinegar
2 teaspoons caster/granulated
   sugar
sea salt and ground black pepper

To assemble
1 par-baked gluten-free baguette
   or small loaf
1 spring onion/scallion, finely
   chopped
1 tablespoon fresh mint, finely
   chopped
1 tablespoon fresh basil, finely
   chopped
1 tablespoon olive oil
freshly squeezed juice of 1 lime
a handful of baby spinach leaves
chargrilled peppers preserved
   in oil, thinly sliced
200 g/7 oz. buffalo mozzarella,
   thinly sliced
15–20 pitted black olives
sea salt and ground black pepper

Serves 2

This pizza is unconventional as it contains no tomatoes, but with fragrant rosemary and crisp thin potato slices, it is no less satisfying than a regular pizza. It is a great accompaniment to serve with barbecued food in the summer, but is also delicious served with a simple salad.

potato & rosemary pizza

For the pizza base

150 ml/⅔ cup warm milk

1 tablespoon fast-action dried yeast

1 tablespoon caster sugar

300 g/2⅓ cups gluten-free strong white bread flour

1 teaspoon baking powder

1 teaspoon xanthan gum

1 teaspoon salt

1 egg

60 ml/¼ cup olive oil

80 ml/⅓ cup plain set yogurt

1 teaspoon finely chopped fresh rosemary

yellow cornflour/fine cornmeal or gluten-free flour, for dusting

For the topping

1 garlic clove, thinly sliced

60 ml/¼ cup olive oil

1 large potato

a few sprigs of fresh rosemary

sea salt and cracked black pepper

2 tablespoons grated Parmesan

a silicone mat (optional)

a large baking sheet

a mandolin (optional)

Serves 4

Put the warm milk, yeast and sugar in the jug/pitcher and leave in a warm place for about 10 minutes until the yeast has activated and a thick foam has formed on top of the liquid.

Sift the flour, baking powder and xanthan gum into a large mixing bowl and add the salt, egg, olive oil, yogurt, chopped rosemary and the yeast mixture. Stir everything together with a wooden spoon until well incorporated and you have a soft dough. Knead the dough a little with your hands and form it into a smooth ball, dusting with a little flour if the dough is too sticky.

Dust a sheet of baking paper or a silicone mat with a little cornflour/cornmeal. Roll out the dough thinly on the paper or mat to a large circle measuring about 30 cm/12 inches in diameter. Slide the dough onto a baking sheet, paper or silicone mat and all, and leave it in a warm place to prove for about 45–60 minutes until it becomes puffy. Preheat the oven to 190°C (375°F) Gas 5.

For the topping, put the garlic and olive oil in a saucepan set over a gentle heat and cook until the garlic turns lightly golden brown, then leave to cool. Once cool, use a pastry brush to brush the top of the pizza with some of the garlic-infused oil.

Slice the potato very thinly – this is best done on a mandolin. (You can peel the potato if you wish but I prefer to leave the skins on as they give a prettier pattern.) Lay the potato slices on top of the pizza, overlapping them slightly. Sprinkle with rosemary, sea salt and pepper and brush the top with more of the garlic oil. Sprinkle the pizza with the Parmesan and bake in the preheated oven for 20–25 minutes until the dough is crisp and the potatoes are cooked and golden brown. Serve straight away.

Calzone are Italian stuffed pizzas. You can vary the fillings – peppers, sun-dried tomatoes and cooked chicken in BBQ sauce all work well. Gluten-free pizza dough can be fragile, so take care when folding the calzone shape and only fill the calzone once the dough has proved.

calzone

Put the warm milk, yeast and sugar in a jug/pitcher and leave in a warm place for about 10 minutes until the yeast has activated and a thick foam has formed on top of the liquid.

Sift the flour, baking powder and xanthan gum into a large mixing bowl. Add the salt, egg, olive oil and yogurt and the yeast mixture, and stir together with a wooden spoon until everything is incorporated and you have a soft dough. Knead the dough a little with your hands and form it into a smooth ball, dusting with a little flour if the dough is too sticky.

Dust a sheet of baking paper or a silicone mat with a little cornflour/cornmeal. Roll out the dough thinly on the baking paper to a large circle measuring about 30 cm/12 inches in diameter. Slide the dough onto a baking sheet, paper or silicone mat and all, and leave it in a warm place to prove for about 45–60 minutes until it becomes puffy.

Preheat the oven to 180°C (350°F) Gas 4.

Spread the passata/crushed tomatoes over half of the dough leaving a small gap around the edge. Lay the mozzarella slices on top of the passata/crushed tomatoes and top with the salami, basil and sliced mushrooms. Wet the bare edges of the dough with a little water. Using the baking paper or silicone mat, lift the un-topped dough half over the filling so that the filling is completely covered and you have a semi-circle shaped calzone. Press the edges together tightly. As the gluten-free dough can be fragile a few cracks may appear on top of the dough, but do not worry as these will be covered by the cheese. Sprinkle the grated mozzarella over the top of the calzone and bake in the preheated oven for 20–25 minutes until the dough is golden brown. Serve straight away.

For the pizza dough

150 ml/²⁄₃ cup warm milk

1 tablespoon fast-action dried yeast

1 tablespoon caster/granulated sugar

300 g/2¹⁄₃ cups gluten-free strong white bread flour, sifted

1 teaspoon baking powder

1 teaspoon xanthan gum

1 teaspoon salt

1 egg

60 ml/¼ cup olive oil

80 ml/¹⁄₃ cup plain set yogurt

yellow cornflour/fine cornmeal or gluten-free flour, for dusting

For the filling

100 g/scant 1 cup passata/ crushed, strained tomatoes

125 g/4 oz. ball of mozzarella, sliced

50 g/2 oz. Napoli salami, cut into strips

1 tablespoon finely chopped fresh basil

30 g/1 oz. button mushrooms, finely sliced

For the topping

50 g/½ cup grated mozzarella

a silicone mat (optional)

Serves 4

There are few better comfort foods than pizza – the Italians have it so right! A crisp pizza base topped with rich tomato and bubbling cheese, this pizza is perfect for a supper with friends, whether they are allergic to gluten or not. They won't be able to tell the difference.

margherita pizza

For the pizza base

100 ml/6½ tablespoons warm milk

1 tablespoon fast-action dried yeast

1 tablespoon caster/granulated sugar

250 g/2 cups gluten-free strong white bread flour

1 egg

2 teaspoons dried mixed herbs

½ teaspoon salt

80 ml/⅓ cup olive oil

For the topping

200 g/¾ cup tomato passata/ crushed, strained tomatoes

200 g/2 cups grated Cheddar cheese

sea salt and ground black pepper

a large baking sheet greased with olive oil

Serves 4

Put the warm milk, yeast and sugar in the jug/pitcher and leave in a warm place for about 10 minutes until the yeast has activated and a thick foam has formed on top of the liquid.

Sift the flour into a large mixing bowl and mix in the egg, yeast mixture, dried herbs, salt and 60 ml/¼ cup of the olive oil with your hands until you have a smooth soft dough. Work the dough into a ball, then add the remaining olive oil to the bowl and roll the dough in the oil until it is absorbed.

Transfer the dough to the prepared baking sheet and press it out into a large circle using your fingertips. Leave the dough in a warm place to prove for 1 hour until the dough becomes puffy.

Preheat the oven to 180°C (350°F) Gas 4.

Spoon the passata/crushed tomatoes onto the dough and smooth out into a thin layer using a spatula or spoon. Sprinkle with the grated cheese, season with a little salt and pepper and bake in the preheated oven for 15–20 minutes until the dough is crisp and the cheese is melted and golden brown. Serve straight away.

These little loaves are served in their pumpkin shells, giving you a perfect combination of roasted pumpkin flesh and wholesome loaf. The bread is made with pumpkin purée so is a wonderful orange colour. They are ideal to serve with soups and casseroles.

pumpkin loaves

Preheat the oven to 180ºC (350ºF) Gas 4.

Cut the tops off the pumpkins and discard the tops. Put the pumpkins in a roasting pan and drizzle with olive oil. Put them in the preheated oven and roast for about 30–40 minutes until the flesh is soft but the pumpkins still hold their shape. Remove from the oven and leave to cool.

When the pumpkin is cool, use a spoon to scoop the flesh and pumpkin seeds from the insides of the pumpkin to hollow out the shells. Discard the seeds (or wash and then roast them in the oven seasoned with salt and pepper for a healthy snack).

Preheat the oven again to 180°C (350°F) Gas 4.

Sift the flour and baking powder (plus xanthan gum, if using) into a large mixing bowl and add the cornmeal and 2 generous tablespoons of the cooked pumpkin flesh. Add the eggs, melted butter, milk and paprika and whisk until you have a smooth mixture. Season with salt and pepper, then divide the mixture between the hollowed out pumpkins and return to the roasting pan. Sprinkle the mixture with pumpkin seeds and drizzle with a little pumpkin seed or olive oil. Bake the pumpkin loaves in the preheated oven for 25–35 minutes until the bread is cooked through.

The loaves are best eaten on the day they are made.

3 small pumpkins

olive oil, for drizzling

100 g gluten-free self-raising flour plus 2 teaspoons baking powder OR ¾ cup gluten-free all-purpose flour plus 3 teaspoons baking powder and ½ teaspoon xanthan gum

100 g/⅔ cup fine cornmeal, plus extra for sprinkling

2 eggs

60 g/4 tablespoons butter, melted and cooled

300 ml/1¼ cups milk

1 teaspoons hot smoked paprika

1 tablespoon pumpkin seeds

pumpkin seed oil, for drizzling

sea salt and ground black pepper

Makes 3 small loaves

Making gluten-free bread dough is very different to regular bread dough. This onion loaf is very easy to prepare and requires no kneading or proving. This bread keeps well if stored in an airtight container and is delicious for sandwiches. You can substitute other toppings in place of the onion and olives, if you prefer.

red onion & olive loaf

250 g gluten-free self-raising flour
   plus 3 teaspoons baking powder
   OR 2 cups gluten-free
   all-purpose flour plus
   5¼ teaspoons baking powder
   and 1½ teaspoons xanthan gum

3 eggs, beaten

50 g/3½ tablespoons butter,
   melted and cooled

300 ml/1¼ cups sour cream

120 g/generous 1 cup grated
   mozzarella cheese

1 generous tablespoon Dijon
   mustard

For the topping

4 red onions, finely sliced

1 tablespoon extra virgin olive oil,
   plus extra for drizzling

1 tablespoon balsamic vinegar

1 tablespoon caster/granulated
   sugar

100 g/⅔ cup pitted black olives

*a 24-cm/10-inch spring-form
cake pan, greased and lined with
non-stick baking paper*

Makes 1 loaf

Begin by preparing the onion topping. Put the sliced onions and olive oil in a frying pan and cook over a gentle heat until the onions are soft and translucent. Add the vinegar and sugar and cook for a few minutes further, until the onions are sticky, then leave to cool.

Preheat the oven to 180°C (350°F) Gas 4.

Sift the flour and baking powder (plus xanthan gum, if using) into a large mixing bowl. Add the beaten eggs, melted butter and sour cream and stir in. Fold in the mozzarella and mustard and mix well, then spoon the mixture into the prepared cake pan. (The mixture will be quite sticky and resemble cake batter rather than traditional bread dough.) Spoon the onions over the top of the bread mixture and sprinkle over the olives. Drizzle the bread with a little more olive oil and bake in the preheated oven for 40–50 minutes until the top is golden and the loaf springs back to your touch. Leave to cool in the pan for 5 minutes and then turn out onto a wire rack to cool completely.

This is a dense loaf with a rich parsnip flavour. Parsnips are my favourite vegetable so, for me, this bread is irresistible. It is great for serving with soups and roasted meat, but does not keep well so needs to be eaten on the day it is made.

parsnip & rosemary bread

Bring a saucepan of salted water to the boil, add the parsnips and cook for about 20 minutes until soft. Drain the parsnips, then mash them with the butter using a potato masher to a smooth purée. Season with black pepper and set aside to cool.

Put the warm water in a jug/pitcher with the yeast and the sugar and leave in a warm place for about 10 minutes, until a thick foam has formed on top of the liquid.

Sift the flour and xanthan gum into the bowl of a stand mixer and stir in the salt and rosemary. Pour in the yeast mixture, add the parsnip purée and mix with a dough hook for 1–2 minutes. Add the oil and a little more warm water (about 50–100 ml/ 3–6 tablespoons), if needed, and mix again until you have a smooth dough.

Dust your hands with flour and bring the dough together into a ball. Place the dough on the prepared baking sheet. Cover with a clean damp cloth and leave to prove for 1½ hours, until the dough has doubled in size.

Preheat the oven to 180°C (350°F) Gas 4.

Brush the top of the loaf with the beaten egg and poke a few rosemary sprigs into the loaf to decorate. Sprinkle the top of the loaf with sea salt flakes, then bake the bread in the preheated oven for 35–45 minutes until golden brown and the loaf sounds hollow when you tap it. Serve warm with butter.

500 g/1 lb. parsnips, peeled and cut into chunks

1 tablespoon butter

100 ml/6½ tablespoons warm water, plus more, if required

7 g/1 envelope fast-action dried yeast

1 tablespoon caster/granulated sugar

550 g/4½ cups gluten-free strong white bread flour, plus extra for dusting

1 teaspoon xanthan gum

1 teaspoon salt

1 tablespoon fresh rosemary, finely chopped

40 ml/3 tablespoons olive oil

1 egg, beaten, to glaze

rosemary sprigs

sea salt flakes and ground black pepper

a stand mixer fitted with a dough hook

a large baking sheet, lined with non-stick baking paper

Makes 1 loaf

This fiery cornbread with a gooey cheese topping is a satisfying snack. A pan of this warm bread is ideal to serve with chilli con carne but is equally lovely eaten just on its own or makes great toasted sandwiches.

cheesy chilli cornbread

For the cornbread

100 g gluten-free self-raising flour
  plus 1 teaspoon baking powder
  OR ¾ cup gluten-free
  all-purpose flour plus
  2 teaspoons baking powder
  and ½ teaspoon xanthan gum

300 g/2 cups fine cornmeal

2 teaspoons bicarbonate of
  soda/baking soda

4 tablespoons chopped fresh
  coriander/cilantro

grated zest of 1 lime

3 spring onions/scallions finely
  chopped

500 ml/2 cups buttermilk

50 g/3½ tablespoons butter,
  melted and cooled

3 eggs

sea salt and ground black pepper

For the cheesy chilli topping

2–3 red chillies, finely sliced

1 tablespoon olive oil

1 tablespoon finely chopped
  coriander/cilantro

2 teaspoons caster/granulated
  sugar

100 g/1 cup grated Cheddar
  cheese

*a 30 x 20-cm/12 x 8-inch baking
pan, greased and lined with
non-stick baking paper*

Makes 1 large loaf

Begin by preparing the topping. Fry the chillies in a saucepan with the olive oil until soft. Season with salt and pepper, add the chopped coriander/cilantro and cook for a few minutes further. Sprinkle over the sugar and cook for a further minute until the chillies start to caramelize, then leave to cool.

Preheat the oven to 190°C (375°F).

Sift the flour and baking powder (plus xantham gum, if using) into a large mixing bowl and stir in the cornmeal, bicarbonate of soda/baking soda, coriander/cilantro, lime zest and spring onions/scallions.

In a separate bowl, whisk together the buttermilk, melted butter and eggs and season with salt and pepper. Add this to the dry ingredients and mix everything together.

Pour the mixture into the prepared baking pan and spread level using a spatula. Sprinkle the grated cheese over the top of the batter, then evenly distribute the chillies. Bake in the preheated oven for 30–35 minutes until the loaf is golden brown on top.

The bread is best served warm on the day it is made.

These delicious Indian breads are a perfect accompaniment to curries and other spiced dishes. Mine are flavoured with black onion seeds but you can add other flavourings of your choosing, such as a little garlic or finely chopped coriander/cilantro.

naan bread

Put the warm milk, yeast and sugar in a jug/pitcher and leave in a warm place for about 10 minutes until a thick foam has formed on top of the liquid.

Sift the flour, baking powder and xanthan gum into a large mixing bowl. Add the salt, egg, yogurt, melted ghee and onion seeds and the yeast mixture and mix well with a wooden spoon until everything is incorporated and you have a soft dough. Divide the dough into 6 portions.

Dust a clean surface generously with yellow cornflour/cornmeal and roll out each portion of dough into an oval shape, dusting the rolling pin with yellow cornflour/cornmeal, too, so that the bread does not stick. Place the rolled out naan breads onto the prepared baking sheets and leave in a warm place for about 45 minutes–1 hour until the naan have risen and are slightly puffy.

Preheat the oven to 200°C (400°F) Gas 6 and place the baking sheets inside. Heat the baking sheets for 5 minutes until they are very hot. Carefully place the naan breads on the baking sheets and cook for 4–5 minutes (you may find it easiest to do this in batches).

Remove the bread from the oven and heat a wok or large frying pan until very hot on the hob/stovetop. Add the naan breads to the pan, one at a time, and cook for a few minutes on each side until the naan have their classic brown spots. (You do not need to add any oil to the pan.) Brush the extra melted ghee over the top of the naan using a pastry brush, if you wish, and serve straight away.

150 ml/⅔ cup warm milk

1 tablespoon fast-action dried yeast

1 tablespoon caster/granulated sugar

300 g/2⅓ cups gluten-free strong white bread flour

1 teaspoon baking powder

1 teaspoon xanthan gum

1 teaspoon salt

1 egg, beaten

125 ml/½ cup set plain yogurt

1 tablespoon ghee (clarified butter), melted and cooled, plus extra for brushing (optional)

scant 1 tablespoon black onion seeds

yellow cornflour/fine cornmeal, for dusting

2 large baking sheets, greased

Makes 6

small bites

These pastries are great to serve with sherry, and you can vary the cheese to any combination of hard cheeses you have in the fridge.

cheese straws

Cut half of butter into small cubes and rub it into the flour using your fingertips or a stand mixer. Add the lemon juice and xanthan gum and mix in. Stir in the cold water, a little at a time (you may not need it all), using a round bladed knife or a stand mixer until you have a soft dough. The dough should be soft but not sticky.

Grate the remaining half of the chilled butter on a coarse grater and keep it chilled until you need it, ideally in the freezer.

Lay a large piece of non-stick baking paper on a clean work surface and dust it with plenty of flour. Transfer the dough onto the baking paper and dust liberally with flour. Use a flour-dusted rolling pin to roll out the pastry to a large rectangle (about 50 x 18 cm/20 x 7 inches). Sprinkle half of the grated butter over the pastry and dust liberally with flour. With one of the shorter edges of the rectangle in front of you, fold the bottom third of the rectangle into the middle so that one third of the pastry is folded over the middle third of the pastry (use the baking paper to help you lift the pastry over). Press the folded pastry down with your hands. Next, take the top third of the pastry and fold it down carefully so it also lies over the middle third. Press down again with your hands. You should now be left with a rectangle measuring about one third of the size that it was.

Dust the surface and rolling pin with flour again, turn the pastry over and roll out into a 50 x 18-cm/20 x 7-inch rectangle again with the folds in the same direction as they were originally rolled (and not rotated as you would with traditional puff pastry). Sprinkle the rolled out pastry with the remaining grated butter, dust again with flour and repeat the folding steps.

Dust the surface and rolling pin again and repeat the rolling out stages twice more (this time without adding any butter but still dusting with flour), each time ensuring that the folds and the direction you are rolling out are the same as this helps the layers to rise. Trim any rough edges and your pastry is ready to use. For best results, use the pastry immediately and do not chill. Preheat the oven to 180°C (350°F) Gas 4.

On a flour-dusted surface, roll out the pastry to a rectangle about 2–3 mm/$\frac{1}{8}$ inch thick, then cut it into 20 rectangles measuring about 12 x 2 cm/5 x $\frac{3}{4}$ inch. Transfer them to the prepared baking sheet using a spatula. Mix together the grated Cheddar and Parmesan and sprinkle it over the pastry. Season with salt and pepper and bake in the preheated oven for 10–15 minutes until the pastry and cheese is golden brown. Leave the straws to cool on the baking sheet before serving.

For the pastry

200 g/1 stick plus 5 tablespoons butter, chilled

175 g/1⅓ cups gluten-free plain/all-purpose flour, sifted, plus extra for dusting

2 teaspoons lemon juice

1 teaspoon xanthan gum

60–80 ml/¼–⅓ cup ice cold water

For the topping

80 g/¾ cup finely grated Cheddar cheese

30 g/⅓ cup finely grated Parmesan cheese

sea salt and ground black pepper

a stand mixer (optional)

a large baking sheet, greased

Makes 20

These small flaky pastry bites make a simple but impressive canapé, topped with roasted tomatoes, mozzarella pearls and fresh basil. As an alternative you could top the tarts with slices of roasted peppers in place of the tomatoes for equally delicious results.

mozzarella & tomato puffs

200 g/1 stick plus 5 tablespoons butter, chilled

175 g/1⅓ cups gluten-free plain/all-purpose flour, sifted, plus extra for dusting

2 teaspoons lemon juice

1 teaspoon xanthan gum

60–80 ml/¼–⅓ cup ice cold water

To assemble

5 tablespoons pesto

16 small cherry tomatoes

32 mozzarella pearls

fresh basil leaves

extra virgin olive oil, for drizzling

sea salt and ground black pepper

a stand mixer (optional)

8-cm/3½-inch and 6-cm/2½-inch round cookie cutters

a large baking sheet, greased and lined with non-stick baking paper

Makes 16

Preheat the oven to 180°C (350°F) Gas 4.

Prepare the pastry according to the instructions for Cheese Straws on page 68, following the method for folding and refolding the pastry, until you reach the point where the pastry is rolled out.

On a flour-dusted surface, roll out the pastry to a rectangle about 2–3 mm/⅛ inch thick. Stamp out 16 rounds with the large pastry cutter and transfer them carefully to the prepared baking sheet.

Using the small cutter, imprint a smaller circle into centre of each pastry round, but do not cut all the way through. Spoon about a teaspoon of pesto into the centre of each pastry round.

Cut the cherry tomatoes in half and place two halves on top of each pastry round, together with two mozzarella pearls. Season with salt and pepper. Bake the puffs in the preheated oven for 10–15 minutes until the pastry is golden brown and the cheese and tomatoes are soft. Sprinkle with basil leaves and drizzle with a little olive oil, to serve.

These dainty crackers are a perfect nibble to serve with drinks. They can be topped with a wide variety of flavourings: I have used salt and pepper, poppy seeds, sesame seeds and piri piri seasoning for some extra heat, but you could try chopped nuts or Chinese five spice, too.

olive oil crackers

Preheat the oven to 200°C (400°F) Gas 6.

Sift the flour and baking powder into a large mixing bowl. Add the olive oil and 100 ml/6½ tablespoons of water and mix to a soft dough. Chill the dough in the refrigerator for 1 hour.

When chilled, roll out the dough on a flour-dusted surface until it is very thin. (It is important to use lots of flour dusted underneath and on top of the dough and also on the rolling pin as the dough can stick easily.) Cut out about 30 circles of the dough using the cutter and place on the prepared baking sheets. Using a pastry brush, brush a generous layer of olive oil over each cracker and sprinkle with salt and pepper, poppy seeds, sesame seeds or the piri piri seasoning.

Bake the crackers in the preheated oven for 6–10 minutes until lightly golden brown. Leave to cool for a few minutes on the baking sheet, then transfer to a wire rack to cool completely.

The crackers will keep for up to 5 days in an airtight container.

200 g/1⅔ cups gluten-free plain/all-purpose flour, plus extra for dusting
1 teaspoon gluten-free baking powder
25 ml/2 tablespoons extra virgin olive oil, plus extra for brushing

To decorate
sea salt flakes and ground black pepper, piri piri seasoning, poppy seeds, sesame seeds

a 6-cm/2½-inch round cookie cutter

2 baking sheets, greased and lined with non-stick baking paper

Makes about 30

Cheese and biscuits/crackers served with a tangy chutney make a great no hassle supper. These biscuits, bursting with Cheddar cheese, are rich and buttery and melt in the mouth. They are quick and easy to prepare and will keep well stored in an airtight container, although they are quite fragile so store them carefully.

cheese biscuits

170 g/1⅓ cups gluten-free plain/
  all-purpose flour, plus extra
  for dusting
115 g/1 stick butter, chilled
  and cubed
100 g/1 cup grated Cheddar
  cheese
a little milk (optional)

a 7.5-cm/3-inch round cookie
cutter

a large baking sheet, greased and
lined with non-stick baking paper

Makes 15

Preheat the oven to 180°C (350°F) Gas 4.

Sift the flour into a large mixing bowl. Rub the butter into the flour with your fingertips until it resembles fine breadcrumbs. Add the cheese and mix together to form a soft dough, adding a little water or milk if the mixture is too dry. Wrap the dough in clingfilm/plastic wrap and chill in the refrigerator for 1 hour.

On a flour-dusted surface, roll out the dough to about 2–3 mm/⅛ inch thick and cut out 15 rounds using the cutter. Arrange the crackers on the baking sheet and bake in the preheated oven for 10–15 minutes until golden brown. Leave to cool on the baking sheet before serving.

75

The humble oatcake is a great store-cupboard standby. They are quick and easy to prepare, keep well and are good to serve with cheese and chutney. They also make a great cheesecake base in the cheesecake recipe on page 132.

oatcakes

Preheat the oven to 180°C (350°F) Gas 4.

Put the oats, flour, bicarbonate of soda/baking soda, salt and sugar in a large mixing bowl. Rub the butter into the oat mixture using your fingertips. Add the milk and bring the mixture together into a firm dough, adding a little more milk if the mixture is too dry.

On a flour-dusted surface, roll out the dough thinly and stamp out circles using the cookie cutter, re-rolling the trimmings as necessary. (You should only re-roll the dough once as it will become crumbly with the extra flour and difficult to roll.)

Arrange the oatcakes on the prepared baking sheet a small distance apart and bake in the preheated oven for 15 minutes, then turn over and cook for a further 5–10 minutes until crisp and lightly golden brown. Leave to cool on the baking sheet for a few minutes, then transfer to a wire rack to cool completely.

The oatcakes will keep for up to 5 days in an airtight container.

200 g/1½ cups gluten-free rolled oats

80 g/⅔ cup gluten-free plain/all-purpose flour, sifted, plus extra for dusting

1 teaspoon bicarbonate of soda/baking soda

1 teaspoon salt

1 teaspoon sugar

80 g/5 tablespoons butter, chilled and cubed

80 ml/⅓ cup warm milk

a 7.5-cm/3-inch round cookie cutter

a baking sheet, greased and lined with non-stick baking paper

Makes 16

These scotch eggs were inspired by Chris Lee, the wonderful head chef at the Bildeston Crown in Suffolk, England. Rather than the traditional sausagemeat, these quails' eggs are wrapped in smoked haddock, then coated in crispy gluten-free breadcrumbs. They make a great snack for picnics, or serve them as an accompaniment to smoked haddock chowder.

smoked haddock scotch eggs

8 quails' eggs

500 ml/2 cups milk

1 garlic clove, peeled and thinly sliced

150 g/5½ oz. potatoes, peeled and quartered

1 sprig of fresh thyme

250 g/9 oz. undyed smoked haddock, deboned

4 slices gluten-free bread

3–4 tablespoons gluten-free plain/all-purpose flour

2 eggs, beaten

vegetable oil, for frying

sea salt and ground black pepper

Makes 8

Bring a pan of water to the boil and gently lower the quail's eggs in. Cook for 2½ minutes, then drain the eggs and submerge in cold water to stop them cooking. Once cool, peel the eggs and set aside.

Put the milk and garlic in a saucepan and bring to the boil. And the potatoes and thyme and poach for 15–20 minutes over a gentle heat until the potatoes are just soft. Add the fish to the pan and poach for 10–15 minutes until cooked through. Take the pan from the heat and remove the fish, leaving the potatoes to cool in the liquid. Remove the skin and any bones from the fish.

Once cool, drain the potatoes, reserving a little of the milk. Remove the thyme sprig, then mash the potatoes. Flake the fish into the potato and mix everything together well. If the mixture is too dry, add a little of the poaching milk. Season with cracked black pepper and a little salt.

Lay a piece of clingfilm/plastic wrap on a clean flat surface. Place a large spoonful of the haddock mixture in the centre of the clingfilm/plastic wrap and press out thinly with the back of a spoon. Place a quails' egg in the centre of the potato and use the clingfilm/plastic wrap to pull the potato up and around to cover the whole egg. Remove the clingfilm/plastic wrap and shape into a ball in your hands. Set aside whilst you repeat the process with the remaining eggs and potato, then chill in the refrigerator for at least 30 minutes.

Blitz the bread to fine crumbs in a food processor, then tip into a bowl. Put the flour in another bowl and put the beaten eggs in a third bowl. Heat the oil in a saucepan until it is hot enough to make a breadcrumb sizzle when dropped into it. Roll a haddock ball in the flour to give it a light dusting, then roll it in the beaten egg and finally in the breadcrumbs to coat. Repeat to coat all of the balls. Add the eggs to the oil pan in batches and cook for about 2–3 minutes until they are golden brown, turning half way through cooking.

The ingredients for these sausage rolls may seem a little unusual but you will have to trust me that the curry spices and mango chutney make them delicious. Topped with onion seeds for added spice, these are great served with a side of cucumber raita or spicy pickles to dip.

spicy sausage rolls

To make the pastry, put the flour, butter and cream cheese in a food processor and blitz until the mixture resembles fine breadcrumbs. Tip into a large mixing bowl and add the egg yolk and mustard, then mix together with your hands to form a soft dough. If the mixture is too dry, add a little water and if it is too sticky, add a little extra flour. Form the dough into a ball, wrap it in clingfilm/plastic wrap and chill in the refrigerator for 1 hour.

To prepare the filling, remove the sausages from their skins and discard the skins. Mix the sausagemeat with the mango chutney and curry powder. Season with salt and pepper, cover with clingfilm/plastic wrap and chill in the refrigerator until needed.

Preheat the oven to 180°C (350°F) Gas 4.

Divide the chilled pastry into 2 portions. On a flour-dusted surface, roll out each portion to a rectangle measuring about 30 x 18 cm/12 x 7 inches and 2 mm/⅛ inch thick. Divide the sausage mixture in two and shape each portion into a long sausage. Take one of the pastry rectangles and place the sausage mixture down the centre of the long length. Wet both long edges of the rectangle with a little water and fold one of the halves over the sausagemeat so that it meets the pastry edge on the other side. Press down with your fingertips to seal in the sausagemeat. Trim any excess pastry from the long edge with a sharp knife and crimp with a fork. Cut the slice into 6 sausage rolls, then place them on the prepared baking sheet. Repeat with the other pastry rectangle and the remaining sausagemeat. Brush the top of each sausage roll with egg and sprinkle with onion seeds. Bake in the preheated oven for 25–30 minutes until the pastry is golden brown and the sausagemeat is cooked through.

You can eat these wraps hot or cold and they will keep for up to 3 days in an airtight container in the refrigerator.

For the pastry
180 g/1½ cups gluten-free plain/ all-purpose flour, sifted, plus extra for dusting
80 g/5 tablespoons butter, chilled
1 tablespoon cream cheese
1 egg yolk
1 teaspoon gluten-free Dijon mustard

For the filling
400 g/14 oz. gluten-free pork sausages
1 tablespoon mango chutney
1–2 teaspoons hot curry powder
sea salt and ground black pepper

To glaze
1 egg, beaten
black onion seeds, for sprinkling

a baking sheet, greased and lined with non-stick baking paper

Makes 12

My lovely friend and edible flower expert Kathy Brown and I enjoy demonstrating together, and these pretty canapé mushrooms are one of our favourite recipes. Topped with pretty thyme flowers (or just small sprigs of thyme), they are quick and easy to prepare and make a great nibble to serve at parties.

thyme flower mushrooms

20 small open capped mushrooms

3 slices gluten-free bread

50 g/⅓ cup cranberries

1 garlic clove

1 teaspoon thyme leaves

45 ml/3 tablespoons olive oil, plus extra for drizzling

sea salt and ground black pepper

a few thyme flowers or small sprigs of thyme, to garnish (optional)

Makes 20

Preheat the oven to 180°C (350°F) Gas 4.

Remove the stalks of the mushrooms and brush the caps clean with paper towels to remove any dirt. Put the mushroom caps in a roasting pan.

Put the mushroom stalks, bread, cranberries, garlic clove, thyme leaves and olive oil in a food processor and blitz to fine crumbs, then season with salt and pepper. Place a spoonful of the crumbs into each mushroom cap and drizzle with extra olive oil.

Bake the mushrooms in the preheated oven for 15–20 minutes, until the crumbs are crisp and the mushrooms softened. Sprinkle with thyme flowers or a few small sprigs of thyme, to garnish, and serve warm.

I love a good sausage roll. My recipe includes grated apple to keep the meat moist and is encased in a mustard pastry. You can buy sausagemeat in supermarkets, but it often contains gluten so I use gluten-free sausages, removing the skins before using.

pork & apple sausage rolls

For the pastry, rub the butter into the flour with your fingertips. Add the mustard, cream cheese and egg yolk and mix together to form a soft dough, adding a little water if the mixture is too dry. Bring the dough together into a ball, wrap in clingfilm/ plastic wrap and chill in the refrigerator for 1 hour.

To prepare the filling, cook the onion in the olive oil until soft and translucent, then set aside to cool.

Remove the sausages from their skins and discard the skins. Peel and core the apple and grate it into the sausagemeat. Add the onion and mix until everything is incorporated – this is best done with your hands – and season with salt and pepper. Cover and chill in the refrigerator until you are ready to assemble the sausage rolls.

Preheat the oven to 180°C (350°F) Gas 4.

Remove the pastry from the refrigerator and divide it into two portions. On a flour-dusted surface, roll out each portion to a rectangle measuring about 30 x 18 cm/ 12 x 7 inches. Divide the sausage mixture in two and shape each portion into a long sausage. Take one of the pastry rectangles and place the sausage mixture down the centre of the long length. Wet both long edges of the rectangle with a little water and fold one of the halves over the sausagemeat so that it meets the pastry edge on the other side (this is easiest done on a sheet of non-stick baking paper, using the paper to help you lift the pastry over as the pastry is fragile). Press down with your fingertips to seal in the sausagemeat. Trim any excess pastry from the long edge with a sharp knife and crimp with your fingers. Cut the slice into 6 sausage rolls and place them on the prepared baking sheet. Repeat with the other pastry rectangle and the remaining sausagemeat. Pinch together any cracks in the pastry that may appear and cut two small slits into the top of the sausage rolls to let air escape. Whisk together the egg and mustard and brush over the tops of the sausage rolls. Sprinkle with a little cracked black pepper and bake in the preheated oven for 25–30 minutes until the pastry is golden brown and the sausagemeat is cooked through.

You can serve the sausage rolls hot or cold and they will keep for up to 3 days in an airtight container in the refrigerator.

For the pastry

80 g/5 tablespoons butter, chilled

180 g/1⅓ cups gluten-free plain/ all-purpose flour, sifted, plus extra for dusting

1 teaspoon gluten-free Dijon mustard

1 tablespoon cream cheese

1 egg yolk

¼ teaspoon salt

For the filling

1 small onion, finely diced

1 tablespoon olive oil

400 g/14 oz. gluten-free pork sausages

1 small apple

sea salt and ground black pepper

To glaze

1 egg, beaten

2 teaspoons Dijon mustard

cracked black pepper

a baking sheet, greased and lined with non-stick baking paper

Makes 12

These light choux buns are great to serve as canapés. Filled with a goats' cheese cream and topped with crispy bacon and cheese, they are truly delicious. Once you have mastered choux pastry, you can vary the filling – prawn/shrimp and avocado mousse, smoked salmon and cream cheese, creamy mushrooms – the possibilities are endless!

cheese & bacon choux buns

For the buns

65 g/½ cup gluten-free plain/
  all-purpose flour
50 g/3½ tablespoons butter
2 large eggs
30 g/⅓ cup finely grated
  Emmenthal cheese
25 g/1 oz. crispy cooked smoked
  bacon, finely chopped

For the filling

150 g/5½ oz. soft goats' cheese
300 ml/1¼ cups double/heavy
  cream
sea salt and ground black pepper
1 tablespoon snipped chives

*a baking sheet, greased and lined
with non-stick baking paper*

*2 piping bags fitted with large
round nozzles/tips*

Makes 20

Preheat the oven to 200°C (400°F) Gas 6.

Sift the flour twice to remove any lumps. Heat the butter in a saucepan with 150 ml/⅔ cup water until the butter is melted, then bring to the boil. Add all the flour quickly and remove the pan from the heat. Beat hard with a wooden spoon until the dough forms a ball and no longer sticks to the sides of the pan. Leave to cool for about 5 minutes. Whisk the eggs, then beat them into the flour mixture, a little amount at a time, using a balloon whisk. The mixture will form a sticky paste which holds its shape when you lift the whisk up.

Spoon the batter into one of the piping bags and pipe 20 balls of choux pastry onto the prepared baking sheet. With clean hands, wet your finger and smooth down any peaks from the piping so that the pastry is smooth. Sprinkle the tops of the buns with the grated cheese and bacon bits, then bake in the preheated oven for 12–15 minutes. Remove from the oven and use a sharp knife to cut a small slit in each bun to allow the steam to escape, then return the buns to the oven for about 5 minutes until crisp. Leave to cool on a wire rack, then cut the buns in half.

For the filling, whisk together the goats' cheese and cream until the mixture comes into soft peaks. Season well with salt and pepper, then fold through the snipped chives. Spoon the mixture into the other piping bag and pipe a little of the cheese mixture into each choux bun. Serve straight away once filled.

My mum used to make these rolls for picnics when we were little and they were one of my favourite things to eat when we were growing up. They are very simple to prepare and the gooey cheese makes the bread a tasty case for the sausages. Serve with ketchup if you wish.

cheesy sausage parcels

Preheat the oven to 180°C (350°F) Gas 4.

Cut the crusts away from each slice of bread and discard. Roll each slice of bread thinly using a rolling pin on a clean surface.

Mix the grated cheese into the butter, along with the mustard, and season with salt and pepper. Spread a generous layer of the butter mixture over each slice of bread, leaving a strip along one edge uncovered by the butter, then place a sausage along the opposite edge of the bread to this bare strip. Roll up the bread slice so that the sausage is encased in the bread and the bare edge ends up on top. Secure in place with a cocktail stick/toothpick. Repeat with all the remaining bread slices and sausages, placing them on the prepared baking sheet as you go. Bake in the preheated oven for 25–30 minutes until the sausages are cooked through and the bread is golden brown. You do not need to add any oil to the pan as the sausage parcels will cook in the butter. Once cooked, remove from the baking sheet straight away and leave to cool on a wire rack.

You can eat the parcels hot or cold and they will keep for up to 2 days in an airtight container in the refrigerator.

12 slices gluten-free bread
200 g/2 cups grated Cheddar cheese
200 g/1¾ sticks butter, softened
2 teaspoons wholegrain mustard
12 gluten-free chipolata/thin sausages
sea salt and ground black pepper

cocktail sticks/toothpicks

a baking sheet, greased and lined with non-stick baking paper

Makes 12

pies & tarts

This rich indulgent tart, flavoured with hints of truffle and creamy wild mushrooms, is a great supper dish or could be served as part of a sophisticated buffet lunch.

truffle & wild mushroom tart

Begin by preparing the filling as the mushrooms need to cool before being used in the tart. Drain the soaked porcini mushrooms and chop into small pieces, rinsing to remove any grit.

Melt the butter in a large frying pan and add the fresh mushrooms, rehydrated porcini, whole garlic cloves, rosemary and thyme. Cook over gentle heat for about 5 minutes until the mushrooms are soft and smell earthy. Season with truffle salt and pepper and leave to cool.

To make the pastry, rub the butter into the flour using your fingertips, then add the cream cheese, truffle oil and salt and bring together into a soft ball of dough, adding 1–2 tablespoons water if the mixture is too dry. Wrap the pastry dough in clingfilm/plastic wrap and chill in the refrigerator for 1 hour.

On a flour-dusted surface, roll out the pastry to a large rectangle just bigger than the size of the tart pan and use it to line the pan. Press the pastry in firmly with your fingers and trim away any excess using a sharp knife. If the pastry breaks, don't worry, just patch any holes with the pastry trimmings. Prick the base with the prongs of a fork and chill in the refrigerator for a further 30 minutes.

Preheat the oven to 180°C (350°F) Gas 4.

Line the pastry case with non-stick baking paper, fill with baking beans and bake for about 15–20 minutes until the pastry is golden brown. Remove the tart case from the oven and leave to cool slightly. Remove the baking paper and baking beans. Turn the oven temperature down to 120°C (250°F) Gas ½.

Whisk together the whole eggs, egg yolks and cream, season with the truffle salt and pepper, then pour the mixture into the pastry case. Remove the garlic cloves and rosemary and thyme sprigs from the mushroom mixture, then sprinkle the mushrooms over the filling – they will sink into the filling slightly but will still be visible on top. Carefully transfer the tart to the oven and bake for about 1½ hours until the top of the tart is lightly golden brown and the filling is just set with a slight wobble in the centre. Leave to cool and then chill in the refrigerator until you are ready to serve.

The tart will keep for up to 3 days in the refrigerator in an airtight container or covered in clingfilm/plastic wrap.

For the pastry

75 g/5 tablespoons butter, chilled and cubed

190 g/1½ cups gluten-free plain/all-purpose flour, sifted, plus extra for dusting

75 g/5 tablespoons cream cheese

1 tablespoon truffle oil

¼ teaspoon salt

For the mushroom filling

25 g/1 oz. dried porcini mushrooms, soaked in hot water

50 g/3½ tablespoons butter

375 g/13 oz. mushrooms (such as button and chestnut/cremini), roughly chopped

2 garlic cloves, peeled

1 sprig of fresh rosemary

3 sprigs of fresh thyme

2 whole eggs, plus 3 egg yolks

400 ml/1⅔ cups double/heavy cream

truffle salt (or if not available regular sea salt) and ground black pepper

a 25-cm/10-inch loose-based tart pan, greased

baking beans

Serves 8

When asparagus is in first season, this tart is perfect to make the most of this delicious vegetable. With a lemon cream filling and cream cheese pastry, this tart makes an elegant supper dish.

asparagus tart

For the pastry

75 g/5 tablespoons butter, chilled
    and cubed
190 g/1½ cups gluten-free plain/
    all-purpose flour, sifted, plus
    extra for dusting
75 g/5 tablespoons cream cheese
¼ teaspoon salt

For the filling

250 g/9 oz. asparagus
5 egg yolks
300 ml/1¼ cups whipping cream
grated zest of 1 lemon
sea salt and ground black pepper

*a 30 x 18-cm/12 x 7-inch
loose-based tart pan, greased*

baking beans

Serves 8

Trim any woody ends from the asparagus spears, then blanch them in a pan of boiling, salted water for about 3 minutes until just soft. Plunge into iced water and leave until you are ready to fill the tart.

To make the pastry, rub the butter into the flour using your fingertips, then add the cream cheese and salt and bring together into a soft ball of dough, adding 1–2 tablespoons water if the mixture is too dry. Wrap the pastry dough in clingfilm/plastic wrap and chill in the refrigerator for 1 hour.

On a flour-dusted surface, roll out the pastry to 2–3 mm/⅛ inch thick and use it to line the tart pan. Press the pastry in firmly with your fingers and trim away any excess using a sharp knife. If the pastry breaks, don't worry, just patch any holes with the pastry trimmings. Prick the base and chill in the refrigerator for a further 30 minutes.

Preheat the oven to 180°C (350°F) Gas 4.

Line the pastry case with non-stick baking paper, fill with baking beans and bake for about 15–20 minutes until the pastry is golden brown. Remove the tart case from the oven and leave to cool slightly. Remove the baking paper and baking beans. Turn the oven temperature down to 120°C (250°F) Gas ½.

Whisk together the egg yolks, cream and lemon zest and season with salt and pepper, then slowly pour the mixture into the pastry case. Arrange the asparagus spears in a decorative pattern in the tart. They will sink into the filling slightly but will still be visible on top. Carefully transfer the tart to the oven and bake for about 1½ hours until the top of the tart is lightly golden brown and the filling is just set with a slight wobble in the centre. Leave to cool, then chill in the refrigerator until you are ready to serve.

The tart will keep for up to 3 days in the refrigerator in an airtight container or covered in clingfilm/plastic wrap.

My friend Greg Thomas makes the best leek tart. This is my gluten-free version, laden with butter and cream, so best to serve with a salad to counter the calories!

creamy leek tart

Begin by preparing the leeks as they need to cool before being used in the filling. Peel and slice the leeks into small rings. Put them in a saucepan with the butter and season with salt and pepper. Cook over a gentle heat for 15–20 minutes until soft and starting to caramelize but not brown. Set aside to cool.

To make the pastry, rub the butter into the flour using your fingertips, then add the salt and cheese and bring together into a soft ball of dough, adding 1–2 tablespoons water if the mixture is too dry. Wrap the dough in clingfilm/plastic wrap and chill in the refrigerator for 1 hour.

On a flour-dusted surface, roll out the pastry to 2–3 mm/⅛ inch thick and use it to line the tart pan. Press the pastry in firmly with your fingers and trim away any excess using a sharp knife. If the pastry breaks, don't worry, just patch any holes with the pastry trimmings. Prick the base and chill in the refrigerator for a further 30 minutes. Preheat the oven to 180°C (350°F) Gas 4.

Line the pastry case with non-stick baking paper, fill with baking beans and bake for about 15–20 minutes until the pastry is golden brown. Remove the tart case from the oven and leave to cool slightly. Remove the baking paper and baking beans. Turn the oven temperature down to 120°C (250°F) Gas ½.

Spoon three-quarters of the cooled leeks into the pastry case (reserving a quarter of the leeks for the topping) and spread evenly. Whisk together the egg yolks and cream in a jug/pitcher and season with salt and pepper. Slowly pour the cream mixture over the leeks in the tart shell, then spoon the remaining leeks over the top of the tart. Carefully transfer the tart to the oven and bake for about 1½ hours until the top of the tart is lightly golden brown and set with a slight wobble in the centre. Leave to cool and then chill in the refrigerator until you are ready to serve.

The tart will keep for up to 3 days in the refrigerator in an airtight container or covered in clingfilm/plastic wrap.

For the pastry
80 g/5 tablespoons butter, chilled
180 g/1½ cups gluten-free plain/all-purpose flour, sifted, plus extra for dusting
½ teaspoon salt
100 g/1 cup grated Cheddar cheese

For the leek filling
800 g/1 lb. 12 oz. leeks
100 g/6½ tablespoons butter
6 egg yolks
350 ml/1½ cups double/heavy cream
sea salt and ground black pepper

a 25-cm/10-inch tart pan, greased

baking beans

Serves 8

Quiche Lorraine is a classic French tart; smoked bacon and onions surrounded by a rich and creamy egg custard. Although purists may object, I like to add sweetcorn and Cheddar cheese for extra flavour and texture, but you can omit these if you wish. This is a great lunch dish served with potato salad and green leaves.

quiche lorraine

For the pastry

90 g/6 tablespoons butter, chilled

190 g/1½ cups gluten-free plain/ all-purpose flour, sifted, plus extra for dusting

1 egg yolk

1 tablespoon cream cheese

¼ teaspoon salt

1 teaspoon cracked black pepper

1–2 tablespoons milk (optional)

For the filling

1 large onion, finely sliced

1 tablespoon olive oil

240 g/9 oz. streaky/fatty bacon, cut into small strips

3 eggs, plus 2 egg yolks

300 ml/1¼ cups double/heavy cream

140 g (drained weight)/1 cup sweetcorn/corn kernels

60 g/a generous ½ cup grated Cheddar cheese

sea salt and ground black pepper

a 30 x 20-cm/12 x 8-inch loose-based tart pan, greased

baking beans

Serves 8

For the filling, put the sliced onion and olive oil in a frying pan and cook over a medium heat. Once the onion starts to soften, add the bacon to the pan and fry until the bacon is cooked and starts to turn light golden brown at the edges. Remove from the heat and leave to cool.

To make the pastry, rub the butter into the flour using your fingertips, then add the egg yolk, cream cheese, salt and pepper. Bring the dough together into a soft ball, adding 1–2 tablespoons milk if the mixture is too dry. Wrap the pastry dough in clingfilm/plastic wrap and chill in the refrigerator for 1 hour.

On a flour-dusted surface, roll out the pastry to a large rectangle just bigger than the size of the tart pan and use it to line the pan. Press the pastry in firmly with your fingers and trim away any excess using a sharp knife. If the pastry breaks, don't worry, just patch any holes with the pastry trimmings. Chill the pastry case in the refrigerator for 30 minutes.

Preheat the oven to 180°C (350°F) Gas 4.

Line the pastry case with non-stick baking paper, fill with baking beans and bake for about 15–20 minutes until the pastry is golden brown. Remove the tart case from the oven and leave to cool slightly. Remove the baking paper and baking beans. Turn the oven temperature down to 140°C (275°F) Gas 1.

Whisk together the eggs, egg yolks and cream, then stir in the onion and bacon, sweetcorn/corn and grated cheese and season with salt and pepper. Pour the mixture into the baked pastry case and bake the quiche for about 1½ hours until the filling is just set but still has a slight wobble in the centre. Leave to cool, then chill in the refrigerator until you are ready to serve.

The quiche will keep for up to 2 days in the refrigerator in an airtight container or covered in clingfilm/plastic wrap.

Although avocado is most often served cold in salads, it is delicious when baked. You need to ensure that it is thoroughly coated in lemon juice so that it does not discolour in the tart. This is a rich tart and is perfect to serve at Christmas with a glass of prosecco or Champagne.

smoked salmon & avocado flan

To make the pastry, rub the butter into the flour using your fingertips, then mix in the lemon zest, salt, egg yolk and cream cheese. Bring together to a soft dough with your hands, adding 1–2 tablespoons milk if the mixture is too dry. Wrap the pastry dough in clingfilm/plastic wrap and chill in the refrigerator for 1 hour.

On a flour-dusted surface, roll out the pastry to a circle just bigger than the size of the tart pan and use it to line the pan, trimming away any excess using a sharp knife. If the pastry breaks, don't worry, just patch any holes with the pastry trimmings. Chill the pastry case in the refrigerator for 30 minutes.

Preheat the oven to 180°C (350°F) Gas 4.

Line the pastry case with non-stick baking paper, fill with baking beans and bake for about 15–20 minutes until the pastry is golden brown. Remove the tart case from the oven and leave to cool slightly. Remove the baking paper and baking beans. Turn the oven temperature down to 110°C (225°F) Gas ¼.

For the filling, peel the avocados and remove the pits. Cut them into thin slices and coat very well in the lemon juice to prevent them turning brown.

In a large mixing bowl, whisk together the egg yolks and cream, then add the avocado and lemon juice, and the salmon and season with pepper. (You do not need to add any salt as the smoked salmon is sufficiently salty.) Pour the mixture into the baked pastry case and bake for about 1½ hours until the filling is just set but still has a slight wobble in the centre. Leave to cool, then chill in the refrigerator until you are ready to serve.

The tart needs to be eaten on the day it is made as the avocado can discolour.

For the pastry
90 g/6 tablespoons butter, chilled and cubed
190 g/1½ cups gluten-free plain/all-purpose flour, sifted, plus extra for dusting
grated zest of 1 lemon
¼ teaspoon salt
1 egg yolk
1 tablespoon cream cheese
1–2 tablespoons milk (optional)

For the filling
2 small ripe avocados
freshly squeezed juice of 2 lemons
5 egg yolks
300 ml/1¼ cups double/heavy cream
180 g/6 oz. smoked salmon, cut into strips
freshly ground black pepper

a 25-cm/10-inch loose-based tart pan, greased

baking beans

Serves 8–10

For the vegetable filling

3 carrots, peeled and finely
    chopped

2 parsnips, peeled and finely
    chopped

1 swede/rutabaga, peeled
    and finely chopped

50 g/3½ tablespoons butter

2 bay leaves

125 ml/½ cup white wine

For the pastry

90 g/6 tablespoons butter, chilled

190 g/1½ cups gluten-free
    plain/all-purpose flour, sifted,
    plus extra for dusting

1 tablespoon cream cheese

60 g/generous ½ cup grated
    Cheddar cheese

¼ teaspoon salt

For the sauce

½ onion, finely chopped

250 ml/1 cup white wine

1 bay leaf

200 ml/¾ cup vegetable stock

150 ml/⅔ cup double/heavy
    cream

1 teaspoon gluten-free Dijon
    mustard

sea salt and ground black pepper

For the topping

550 g/1 lb. 4 oz. potatoes

80 g/5 tablespoons butter

120 ml/½ cup milk

2 egg yolks

3 tablespoons grated Cheddar
    cheese

4 x 13-cm/5-inch loose-based tart
pans (3 cm/1 inch high), greased

baking beans

a piping bag

Makes 4

These golden pies, topped with fluffy mashed potato, are filled with vegetables in a creamy white wine sauce.

golden vegetable pies

To make the filling, put the carrots, parsnips, swede/rutabaga, butter, bay leaves, wine and a little salt in a saucepan with enough water to cover the vegetables and simmer until the vegetables are soft but still hold their shape. Drain, remove the bay leaves, and leave to cool.

To make the pastry, rub the butter into the flour using your fingertips, then mix in the cream cheese, grated Cheddar and the salt and bring together into a soft ball of dough, adding 1–2 tablespoons water if the mixture is too dry. Wrap the pastry dough in clingfilm/plastic wrap and chill in the refrigerator for 1 hour.

Divide the dough into quarters. On a flour-dusted surface, roll out one portion of the pastry to 2–3 mm/⅛ inch thick and use it to line one of the pans. Press the pastry in firmly with your fingers and trim away any excess using a sharp knife. If the pastry breaks, don't worry, just patch any holes with the pastry trimmings. Repeat with the remaining pastry to line the remaining 3 pans. Prick the bases with a fork and chill in the refrigerator for a further 30 minutes.

Preheat the oven to 180°C (350°F) Gas 4.

Line the pastry cases with non-stick baking paper, fill with baking beans and bake them for about 15–20 minutes until the pastry is golden brown. Remove the pastry cases from the oven, leave for about 5 minutes to cool slightly, then remove the paper and baking beans and leave the tart cases in the pans to cool completely.

For the sauce, put the onion, wine and bay leaf in a saucepan and simmer over a gentle heat until the wine has reduced to about a quarter of the original volume of liquid. Add the stock and simmer again until the liquid has reduced by half. Add the cooked vegetables to the pan with the cream and mustard, then season well. Simmer for a few minutes until the sauce thickens slightly, then remove from the heat and leave to cool.

For the potato topping, boil the potatoes in salted water for about 20 minutes until they are soft. Remove from the heat, drain and pass through a sieve/strainer, pressing with the back of a spoon so that you have a smooth potato purée with no lumps. Whilst the potato is still hot, mix in the butter, milk and egg yolks, beating to make a smooth purée.

Preheat the oven again to 180°C (350°F) Gas 4. With the pastry cases still in the pans, fill each case with a few spoonfuls of the vegetable mixture and plenty of sauce until the pastry cases are almost filled. Spoon the potato purée into the piping bag and pipe over the top of the pies, smoothing with a round-bladed knife, then sprinkle each pie with a little grated Cheddar. Bake in the preheated oven for 20–25 minutes until the pies are golden brown on top. Carefully remove the pies from the pans, taking care as the pastry is fragile, and serve straight away.

As an alternative to the popular French sweet dessert tatins, this is a savoury version, packed with butternut squash and warming chilli. It is delicious served warm accompanied by a creamy Greek-style yogurt and a tangy dressed green salad.

butternut squash & chilli tatin

Preheat the oven to 180°C (350°F) Gas 4.

Cut the squash in half and remove the seeds using a spoon, then cut it into 2-cm/1-inch thick slices, leaving the skin on if you wish. Put the squash in a roasting pan and drizzle with the olive oil. Add the thyme, garlic and chillies to the pan, season with salt and pepper and roast for about 40 minutes until the squash is soft but still holds its shape and is starting to caramelize. Remove from the oven and leave to cool slightly. If you are going to be cooking the tart immediately, leave the oven on.

For the glaze, heat together the butter, sugar and vinegar in a small saucepan until thin and syrupy, then pour it into the pan. Scatter the roasted chillies and thyme sprigs on the base of the dish and arrange the roasted butternut squash slices in a pattern on top.

To make the pastry, mix together the flour and suet/vegetable shortening and season with salt and pepper. Add the milk gradually (you may not need it all depending on the absorption rate of your flour, which differs from brand to brand) and bring the mixture together into a soft dough.

Preheat the oven again to 180°C (350°F) Gas 4.

On a flour-dusted surface, roll out the dough to a circle just larger than the size of the pan. Using a rolling pin, gently lift the pastry circle on top of the butternut squash in the pan and press it down tightly. Patch any cracks with pastry trimmings. Bake the tatin in the preheated oven for 20–25 minutes until the pastry is golden brown. Remove from the oven, invert onto a serving plate and serve straight away.

For the squash

1 large butternut squash
80 ml/⅓ cup olive oil
5 sprigs thyme
2 garlic cloves, sliced
2 large red chillies, whole
sea salt and ground black pepper

For the glaze

30 g/2 tablespoons butter
1 tablespoon caster/granulated sugar
1 tablespoon balsamic vinegar

For the pastry

150 g/1 cup plus 2 tablespoons gluten-free plain/all-purpose flour, sifted, plus extra for dusting
90 g gluten-free shredded suet OR 6 tablespoons vegetable shortening, chilled and grated (see page 11)
sea salt and ground black pepper
about 120 ml/½ cup milk

a 20-cm/8-inch tatin pan or cast-iron frying pan, greased

Serves 4–6

Roasted tomatoes and creamy goats' cheese are a winning flavour combination. Encased in a tangy Parmesan pastry crust, these little tarts make a perfect snack. If you prefer, you can make miniature versions in tiny tart cases, topped with just one tomato.

roasted tomato tarts

For the pastry

90 g/6 tablespoons butter, chilled

190 g/1½ cups gluten-free plain/all-purpose flour, sifted, plus extra for dusting

50 g/scant 1 cup grated Parmesan cheese

For the filling

600 g/1 lb. 5 oz. cherry tomatoes on the vine

4–5 sprigs of fresh thyme

2 tablespoons olive oil

1 tablespoon balsamic vinegar

½ tablespoon caster/granulated sugar

200 g/7 oz. creamy goats' cheese or other soft creamy cheese

sea salt and ground black pepper

8 x 10-cm/4-inch loose-based mini tart pans, greased

a pastry cutter slightly bigger than the tart pans

baking beans

Makes 8

To make the pastry, rub the butter into the flour using your fingertips, then mix in the grated Parmesan. Add a tablespoon of water and bring together to a soft dough with your hands, adding a further 1–2 tablespoons water if the mixture is too dry. Wrap the pastry dough in clingfilm/plastic wrap and chill in the refrigerator for 1 hour.

On a flour-dusted surface, roll out the pastry to 2–3 mm/⅛ inch thick and use the pastry cutter to stamp out circles of pastry just larger than the size of your tart pans. Line the pans with the pastry, pressing it in firmly with your fingertips and patching any cracks with the trimmings. Trim away any excess at the edges using a sharp knife. Prick the bases and chill in the refrigerator for a further 30 minutes.

Preheat the oven to 180°C (350°F) Gas 4.

Line the pastry cases with non-stick baking paper, fill with baking beans and bake them for 10–15 minutes until the pastry is golden brown. Leave to cool, but leave the oven on to cook the tomatoes. Once cool, remove the baking paper and baking beans.

Put the tomatoes in a roasting pan with the thyme sprigs and drizzle with the olive oil and balsamic vinegar. Sprinkle over the sugar and season with salt and black pepper. Bake for 15–20 minutes until the tomatoes have softened and are starting to caramelize. Remove from the oven and leave to cool.

Assemble the tarts just before serving. Place a generous spoonful of the cheese in the base of each tart case, top with the roasted tomatoes and short sprigs of the roasted thyme, drizzle with the roasting juices and serve.

The tart cases will keep, unfilled, for up to 3 days in an airtight container.

Samphire is a green sea shrub which is great with any fish as it tastes of the salty sea. Paired here with a smoked salmon mousse and quails' eggs, these tartlets are the perfect canapé to serve with Champagne. If you can't find samphire, they are delicious with watercress, too.

samphire & salmon tartlets

Begin by soft boiling the quails' eggs. Bring a pan of water to the boil and gently lower the eggs in. Cook for 2½ minutes then drain the eggs and submerge in cold water to stop them cooking. Once cool, peel the eggs and set aside.

To make the pastry, mix the flour and cornmeal together in a large mixing bowl. Rub the butter into the flour mixture with your fingertips until the mixture resembles fine breadcrumbs. Mix in the cream cheese, egg yolk and lemon zest and bring the mixture together into a ball, adding 1–2 tablespoons water if the mixture is too dry. Wrap the pastry in clingfilm/plastic wrap and chill in the refrigerator for 30 minutes. Preheat the oven to 180°C (350°F) Gas 4.

On a flour-dusted surface, roll out the pastry to 2–3 mm/⅛ inch thick and cut out 12 circles using the cutter, re-rolling the pastry as needed. Line each hole of the bun pan with a circle of pastry and press in lightly with your finger tips. Patch any cracks using the pastry trimmings. Line each case with a small piece of baking paper and fill with baking beans. Bake in the preheated oven for 8–12 minutes until crisp and golden brown. Leave to cool, then remove the baking beans and baking paper.

For the mousse, put the salmon in a food processor with the lemon and a little freshly ground black pepper and blitz until the salmon is finely chopped. Add the cream and blitz again until the cream thickens and you have a smooth mousse. Store in the refrigerator until you are ready to serve.

Blanche the samphire in boiling water for about 3 minutes, then plunge into iced water so that it retains its colour. Cut the soft-boiled quails' eggs in half.

To assemble, spoon the mousse into the piping bag and pipe a star into each pastry case. If you are not using a piping bag, place a spoonful of the mousse into each case. Lay a few samphire strands on top of the mousse. Cut the smoked salmon into strips and place one on top of each tart, along with half a quails' egg to decorate. Season with a little cracked black pepper and serve straight away.

For the pastry

90 g/¾ cup gluten-free plain/all-purpose flour, sifted, plus extra for dusting

40 g/⅓ cup fine cornmeal

50 g/3½ tablespoons butter, chilled and cubed

1 tablespoon cream cheese

1 egg yolk

grated zest of 1 lemon

For the salmon mousse

100 g/3½ oz. smoked salmon

freshly squeezed juice of 1 lemon

freshly ground black pepper

150 ml/⅔ cup double/heavy cream

To assemble

50 g/2 oz. samphire

2 slices smoked salmon

6 quails' eggs

freshly cracked black pepper

a 12-hole bun pan, greased

an 8-cm/3-inch round fluted cutter

12 small squares of baking paper

baking beans

a piping bag fitted with large star nozzle/tip (optional)

Makes 12

This is a great pie to serve during the festive season, bursting with spices and cranberries and sweetened with a little apple purée. Hot crust pastry works really well in a gluten-free version and you would be able to serve this pie to anyone without them knowing it is gluten free.

apple & cranberry pork pie

For the pastry
300 g/2⅓ cups gluten-free plain/
  all-purpose flour
2 teaspoons gluten-free Dijon
  mustard
1 teaspoon salt
140 g/generous ½ cup lard

For the filling
200 g smoked bacon lardons/
  1 cup thick-sliced back bacon
  cut into cubes
300 g/10½ oz. minced/ground
  pork
200 g/7 oz. fresh pork belly,
  rind trimmed and very finely
  chopped
1 teaspoon ground allspice
2 tablespoons apple sauce
sea salt and ground black pepper

For the topping
250 g/2 cups fresh cranberries
2 tablespoons redcurrant jelly

a 18-cm/7-inch round loose-based
deep cake pan, greased

Preheat the oven to 180°C (350°F) Gas 4.

For the pastry, sift the flour into a large mixing bowl and add the mustard and salt. Heat the lard in a saucepan with 130 ml/½ cup water and bring to the boil, then carefully pour into the flour and beat in with a wooden spoon. Leave to cool for a few minutes, then, while the pastry is still warm, press the pastry into the base and sides of the cake pan evenly so that the pastry comes to the top of the pan sides. Press the edge into a fluted pattern with your fingertips.

In a bowl, mix together the bacon, minced/ground pork and pork belly with the allspice and apple sauce. Season well with salt and pepper and spoon the mixture into the pastry case, pressing in tightly with the back of a spoon, until the pastry case is full to just below the rim of the pastry (you may not need all of the meat). Cover the top of the meat with non-stick baking paper and press down firmly. Bake the pie in the preheated oven for 30 minutes, then turn the temperature down to 150°C (300°F) Gas 2 and bake for a further 2 hours until the juices from the meat run clear, then leave to cool.

For the topping, simmer the cranberries in 100 ml/scant ½ cup of water, seasoned with salt and pepper, until the cranberries are just soft and their skins start to split. Strain the water from the cranberries, leave them to cool slightly, then spoon the cranberries on top of the pie. Heat the redcurrant jelly in a saucepan with 1 tablespoon of water until the jelly has melted and is of a pourable consistency. Spoon over the cranberries and leave to cool.

The pie will store in the refrigerator for up to 3 days in an airtight container.

111

Filled with fillet steaks, pâté, mushroom duxelles and a little brandy
for good measure, these Wellingtons are great for special occasions.

beef wellington

Soak the dried mushrooms in enough boiling water to cover them, add the sherry
and leave to soak for about 20 minutes. Once rehydrated, drain the mushrooms,
squeeze out any liquid, then finely chop them.

Melt the butter in a large frying pan and add the chopped fresh and rehydrated
mushrooms. Season with truffle salt and freshly ground black pepper. Cook the
mushrooms until they are very soft and reduced, then leave to cool completely.

Sprinkle cracked black pepper over the steaks and sear in a hot griddle pan for
about 30 seconds on each side. Using kitchen tongs, brown the sides of the steaks,
too, so that the meat is sealed all over. Remove from the pan and transfer to a plate
to cool. Brush with a tablespoon of brandy and chill until needed.

For the pastry, put the flour and suet/vegetable shortening in a large mixing bowl,
season with salt and pepper, then gradually add enough water (about 120–150 ml/
½–⅔ cup) to bring the mixture together into a soft dough.

On a flour-dusted surface, roll out the dough thinly and cut out 2 circles about
17 cm/7 inches in diameter and 2 about 20 cm/8 inches in diameter (it is easiest to do
this in batches, cutting around dinner plates of the right size). Re-roll the trimmings
and cut out leaves using a sharp knife to decorate the pies with.

Lay the 2 smaller circles of pastry on the baking sheet. Place a spoonful of the
mushroom mixture in the centre of each and place the steaks on top. Cut the pâté
into 2 pieces and place one on top of each steak, smoothing down onto the steak
with a knife. Cover the pâté with the rest of the mushrooms, pressing down firmly.

Brush the around edges of the small circles of pastry with a little cold water.
Carefully lift the larger pastry circles on top of the steak and mushrooms and smooth
down the pastry with your hands so that it sits snugly over the filling. Seal the pastry
edges by crimping them together with your fingers, then trim away any excess pastry.

Beat the egg with the mustard and use a pastry brush to glaze the top of the
pies with it. Arrange the pastry leaves on top of the pies (if any small cracks have
appeared in the pastry, you can use the leaves to cover them) and brush the leaves
with the egg mixture as well. Chill the Wellingtons in the refrigerator until you are
ready to cook.

Preheat the oven to 180°C (350°F) Gas 4 and bake the beef Wellingtons for
20–25 minutes until the pastry is golden brown, then serve straight away.

For the mushroom duxelles
25 g/1 oz. dried wild mushrooms
60 ml/¼ cup sweet sherry
50 g/3½ tablespoons butter
50 g/2 oz. girolles mushrooms,
  finely chopped
50 g/2 oz. trompettes de la mort
  mushrooms, finely chopped
90 g/3 oz. chestnut mushrooms,
  finely chopped
truffle salt (or sea salt and a little
  truffle oil)
freshly cracked black pepper

For the pastry
200 g/1⅔ cups gluten-free plain/
  all-purpose flour, plus extra
  for dusting
100 g gluten-free shredded suet
  OR 6½ tablespoons vegetable
  shortening, chilled and grated
  (see page 11)
sea salt and ground black pepper

To assemble
2 fillet steaks (about 125 g/4½ oz.
  each in weight)
brandy, for brushing
100 g/3½ oz. gluten-free pork
  and mushroom pâté
1 egg, beaten
2 teaspoons gluten-free Dijon
  mustard

*a baking sheet, greased and lined
with non-stick baking paper*

Serves 2

When the weather is cold, there is nothing nicer than tucking into a hearty pie straight from the oven. Beer usually contains gluten, but there is a good variety of gluten-free beers available, which work well in this pie.

beef & ale pie

For the filling

2–3 tablespoons olive oil

1 onion, finely sliced

1 garlic clove, finely sliced

700 g/1½ lb. beef stewing steak

200 g/7 oz. baby carrots

1 leek, sliced and washed

200 g/7 oz. open cap
mushrooms, quartered

500 ml/2 cups gluten-free beer

200 ml/¾ cup beef stock

1 tablespoon cornflour/cornstarch

60 ml/¼ cup brandy

1 tablespoon horseradish sauce

sea salt and ground black pepper

For the pastry

200 g gluten-free self-raising flour
plus 2 teaspoons baking powder
OR 1⅔ cups gluten-free
all-purpose flour plus
3¾ teaspoons baking powder
and 1¼ teaspoons xanthan
gum, plus extra flour for dusting

110 g gluten-free shredded suet
OR 7 tablespoons vegetable
shortening, chilled and grated
(see page 11)

1 tablespoon horseradish sauce

150–250 ml/⅔–1 cup milk

1 egg, beaten

a large flameproof lidded casserole

a 26-cm/10-inch diameter pie dish

a pie funnel

Serves 6

Preheat the oven to 180°C (350°F) Gas 4.

Heat half the oil in the casserole dish and add the onions and garlic. Season with salt and pepper and sauté over a gentle heat until they are soft and a light golden brown colour, then remove them from the pan. Add the remaining oil to the pan and, in batches, brown the meat on all sides, seasoning with salt and pepper. Remove the meat from the pan and drain off any oil. Add the meat, onions and garlic back to the pan along with the carrots, leek, mushrooms, beer and stock. Put the lid on the casserole and transfer it to the preheated oven to cook for about an hour, until the meat is tender.

Remove the pan from the oven and set it on the hob/stovetop to simmer. Remove a ladleful of the stock and stir in the cornflour/cornstarch. Pour it back into the pan and stir in, along with the brandy and horseradish. Stir over the heat until the sauce starts to thicken, then pour into the pie dish and leave to cool.

For the pastry, mix together the flour, baking powder (plus xanthan gum, if using), suet/vegetable shortening and horseradish sauce in a large mixing bowl. Add the milk to the bowl gradually (you may not need it all depending on the absorption rate of your flour, which differs from brand to brand) and bring the mixture together with your hands to form a soft dough that is not sticky.

On a flour-dusted surface, roll out the pastry dough to a circle slightly larger than the size of your pie dish. Place a pie funnel in the middle of the filling in the dish and then cover the dish with the pastry, piercing a hole in the middle so that the pie funnel comes up through the pastry. Crimp the pastry with your fingers around the edge of the dish to seal. Decorate the pie top with any pastry trimmings cut out into the shape of leaves. Brush the top of the pie with beaten egg using a pastry brush and bake in the oven for 25–30 minutes until the pastry crust is golden brown.

The pie is best eaten on the day it is made, although the filling can be made in advance and frozen for up to 1 month.

This comforting winter game pie is made with rich venison, seasoned with juniper berries and sweetened with parsnips.

hunter pie

Put the dried mushrooms in a small bowl and pour over enough boiling water to cover them, then leave them to soak for 20 minutes. Once rehydrated, drain the mushrooms and squeeze out any excess liquid, then roughly chop them with a sharp knife.

Preheat the oven to 180°C (350°F) Gas 4.

Heat half the oil in the casserole pan set over a gentle heat. Add the onion, season with salt and pepper and cook gently until the onion is very soft. Remove the onion from the pan and set aside. Cut the venison into cubes (about 4 cm/1½ inches in size) and season. Heat the remaining oil in the pan and cook the venison, stirring all the time, until the meat is sealed and lightly golden brown. Return the onion to the pan, add the chestnut and rehydrated mushrooms and pour in the red wine and stock. Crush the juniper berries in a pestle and mortar, add to the pan with the bay leaf and simmer the casserole on the hob/stovetop for about 5 minutes. Add the parsnips to the pan, then transfer to the preheated oven and cook for 45 minutes. Turn the temperature down to 150°C (300°F) Gas 2 and cook for a further 1½ hours until the meat is tender. Remove from the oven and leave to cool slightly, then remove the bay leaf. Ladle out a little of the casserole liquid and mix it with the cornflour/cornstarch, then return the liquid to the pan. Stir through to thicken the sauce. Leave the oven on.

For the pastry, mix together the flour, baking powder (plus xanthan gum, if using) and suet/vegetable shortening in a large mixing bowl. In a pestle and mortar, crush the juniper berries with a little salt and pepper, then add to the flour mixture. Add the milk to the bowl gradually (you may not need it all) and bring the mixture together into a soft dough.

On a flour-dusted surface, roll out the dough thinly. Upturn one of the pie dishes onto the pastry sheet and use it as a guide to cut around, making sure you allow enough extra pastry to go up the sides of the pie dishes. Line the pie dish with the pastry, and trim off any excess. Discard any trimmings or use them to cut leaves from to decorate the top of your pies with. Divide the venison mixture between the 4 pie dishes. Place one of the pastry lids on top of each dish and crimp with your fingertips to fit the dish tightly. Brush the tops of the pies with a little beaten egg and cut 2 slits in the top of the pastry to let the air escape. Bake the pies for 20–25 minutes until the pastry is golden brown, then serve.

The pies are best eaten on the day they are made, although the venison pie filling can be made ahead and frozen for up to one month.

For the filling
25 g/1 oz. dried wild mushrooms
2–3 tablespoons vegetable oil
1 onion, thinly sliced
500 g/1 lb. 2 oz. boneless venison leg steak
250 g/9 oz. chestnut mushrooms, quartered
1 x 75 cl bottle red wine
200 ml/¾ cup chicken stock
5 juniper berries
1 bay leaf
5 parsnips, peeled and cut into 5-cm/2-inch chunks
1 tablespoon cornflour/cornstarch
sea salt and ground black pepper

For the pastry
190 g gluten-free self-raising flour plus 1 teaspoon baking powder OR 1½ cups gluten-free all-purpose flour plus 2¾ teaspoons baking powder and 1¼ teaspoons xanthan gum
100 g gluten-free shredded suet OR 6½ tablespoons vegetable shortening, chilled and grated (see page 11)
6 juniper berries
150–180 ml/⅔–¾ cup milk
1 egg, beaten, to glaze

a flameproof lidded casserole

4 small individual pie dishes

Makes 4

baked meals

This spicy chilli is baked with a polenta topping flavoured with lime and coriander/cilantro for a real taste of Mexico. This is really a meal in itself and just needs a spoonful of sour cream and guacamole as an accompaniment. Make sure that the chilli bean sauce is gluten free.

chilli polenta bake

Preheat the oven to 180°C (350°F) Gas 4.

Heat the olive oil in the saucepan set over a gentle heat, add the onion and garlic, season with salt and pepper and cook until lightly golden brown, adding a little water if the onion starts to brown too much. Remove the onion and garlic from the pan and set aside. Add a little further oil to the pan, add the beef and cook until it is browned. Once browned, remove from the pan and drain away any fat. Return the meat, onion and garlic to the pan and add the tomatoes, kidney beans and sauce, tomato purée/paste, brandy, chocolate and paprika and simmer for 10 minutes. Transfer the chilli to the baking dish and bake in the preheated oven for about 45 minutes, until the sauce is rich and thick. Remove the dish from the oven but leave the oven on.

For the topping, put the polenta in a saucepan along with 1 litre/4 cups water and simmer until the polenta is thick and has absorbed all the water (this should take about 3–5 minutes). Stir in the coriander/cilantro, lime zest and crème fraîche and season with salt and pepper.

Spoon the polenta over the top of the chilli, then sprinkle the grated cheese over the top. Bake in the oven for 25–30 minutes until the polenta crust is golden brown. Serve straight away with sour cream and guacamole.

For the chilli

1–2 tablespoons olive oil

1 onion, finely chopped

1– 2 garlic cloves, finely chopped

750 g/1 lb. 10 oz. lean minced/ground beef

a 400-g/14-oz. can pomodorini tomatoes or chopped tomatoes

a 400-g/14-oz. can red kidney beans in chilli sauce

70 g/5 tablespoons tomato purée/paste

60 ml/¼ cup brandy

30 g/1 oz. dark chocolate, chopped

1 teaspoon hot smoked paprika

sea salt and ground black pepper

For the polenta crust

250 g/2 cups polenta express (pre-cooked maize meal)

2 tablespoons chopped fresh coriander/cilantro

grated zest of 1 lime

2 tablespoons crème fraîche or sour cream

80 g/¾ cup grated Cheddar cheese

sour cream, to serve

guacamole, to serve

a baking dish

Serves 6–8

For the meat ragu

1–2 tablespoons olive oil

1 onion, finely chopped

1 garlic clove, finely chopped

1 carrot, peeled, trimmed and grated

750 g/1 lb. 10 oz. lean minced/ground beef

200 g/¾ cup passatta/crushed, strained tomatoes

a 400 g/14 oz. can chopped tomatoes

2 bay leaves

70 g/5 tablespoons double concentrate tomato purée/paste

60 ml/¼ cup brandy

250 ml/1 cup red wine

125 ml/½ cup vegetable stock

For the cheese sauce

50 g/3½ tablespoons butter

1 tablespoon cornflour/cornstarch

500 ml/2 cups warm milk

200 g/2 cups grated Cheddar cheese

a pinch of grated nutmeg

sea salt and ground black pepper

For the pasta

115 g/scant 1 cup yellow cornflour/fine cornmeal

60 g/½ cup quinoa flour

3 eggs, beaten

½ teaspoon salt

gluten-free plain/all-purpose flour, for dusting

a flameproof lidded casserole

a large ovenproof dish

a silicone mat (optional)

Serves 6–8

This delicious lasagne uses a great basic gluten-free pasta recipe that is very useful to have in your repertoire.

lasagne

Preheat the oven to 180°C (350°F) Gas 4.

To make the meat ragu, heat the oil in the casserole pan and add the onion and garlic. Cook until the onion starts to turn a light golden brown and is soft, then add the carrot to the pan and continue to cook for a few minutes until the carrot starts to soften. Remove the onion, garlic and carrot from the pan and set aside. Add a little further oil to the pan and cook the beef in batches until it is browned. Remove from the pan and drain away any fat, then return the meat to the pan with the onion and carrot mixture. Add the passata, tomatoes, bay leaves, tomato purée/paste, brandy, red wine and stock and bring to the boil. Transfer the casserole to the oven and cook for about 1 hour until thickened. Remove any excess oil from the top with a spoon, then let cool.

For the cheese sauce, melt the butter in a saucepan and add the cornflour/cornmeal. Cook for a minute, then gradually add the warm milk, a little at a time, stirring continuously until you have a smooth sauce. Add three quarters of the cheese and stir until melted. Season with a little grated nutmeg, salt and pepper, then set aside until cool. Reserve the remaining cheese to sprinkle over the top of the lasagne.

Preheat the oven to 180°C (350°F) Gas 4. Set a pan of salted water to boil, ready to cook the pasta straight away. Spread half of the meat ragu over the base of your serving dish.

Sift together the yellow cornflour/cornmeal and quinoa flour, then tip it into a mound on a silicone mat or clean work surface. Make a well in the middle and add the eggs and salt. Mix the eggs into the flour with your fingertips until you have a soft dough.

Dust a work surface and a rolling pin with plenty of flour and cut the pasta dough into quarters. Coat liberally in flour and then roll out each quarter, one by one, very thinly. Once rolled out, cut the dough into rectangular sheets measuring about 15 cm x 8 cm/6 x 3½ inches. As soon as they are rolled out, cook the pasta sheets, one at a time for about 2 minutes. When cooked, remove each sheet from the water with a slotted spoon so that the water drains off and lay it on top of the meat. Repeat, rolling out and cooking enough pasta sheets to cover the bottom layer of meat. Cover the pasta with a layer of the cheese sauce and spread out thinly. Continue to roll out and cook more pasta sheets and layer them on top of the cheese sauce until it is completely covered. Spoon the remaining meat ragu on top of the pasta and spread out evenly. Cover with the remaining cheese sauce and top with the reserved grated cheese. Sprinkle a little nutmeg and cracked black pepper over the top of the lasagne, then bake in the preheated oven for about 30–40 minutes until the cheese is golden brown on top. Serve straight away or cook and then chill in the refrigerator for up to 2 days, reheating to serve.

This is a really satisfying dish that is a meal all on its own. It needs no accompaniment, although you could serve it with a salad if you wish. Rich and creamy, this is the ultimate comfort food on a cold winter's evening.

cheese & bacon bread pudding

Preheat the oven to 180°C (350°F) Gas 4.

Put the butter, milk and cream in a saucepan set over a gentle heat, and heat until the butter has melted. Set aside to cool.

Put the bacon lardons/cubes in a frying pan and cook for a few minutes until they have released some oil and are lightly golden brown, then add the onion to the pan and cook until softened. Stir in the sweetcorn/corn kernels and cook for a further 2–3 minutes.

Cut the bread slices into quarters and arrange a layer over the base of the oven dish. Spoon over a little of the bacon and corn mixture, spread evenly, then add another layer of bread. Continue layering up the bread and filling mixture until all the ingredients are used up.

Season the cooled milk mixture with salt and black pepper, then whisk in the eggs. Pour the mixture over the bread filling and sprinkle the cheese over the top. Bake in the preheated oven for 25–30 minutes until golden brown, and serve.

50 g/3½ tablespoons butter

300 ml/1¼ cups milk

300 ml/1¼ cups double/heavy cream

180 g bacon lardons/1 cup thick-sliced back bacon, cut into cubes

1 onion, finely chopped

140 g (drained weight)/⅔ cup sweetcorn/corn kernels

5 slices gluten-free bread (brown or white)

4 eggs, beaten

85 g/¾ cup grated Cheddar cheese

sea salt and ground black pepper

a 25-cm/10-inch oven proof dish, greased

Serves 4

These delicate stuffed pancakes are inspired by my friend
David Gibbs, who makes the best gluten-free pancakes ever.

crespolini

For the tomato sauce

120 ml/½ cup olive oil

1 onion, finely chopped

1 garlic clove, finely sliced

2 x 400 g/14 oz. cans plum
tomatoes

sea salt and ground black pepper

For the béchamel sauce

50 g/3½ tablespoons butter

1 tablespoon cornflour/cornstarch

250 ml/1 cup milk

2 bay leaves

200 ml/¾ cup double/heavy
cream

For the filling

250 g/9 oz. spinach

250 g/9 oz. ricotta

a pinch of freshly grated nutmeg

freshly squeezed juice of 1 lemon

1 teaspoon grated lemon zest

50 g/¾ cup grated Parmesan
cheese, plus extra to sprinkle
on top

For the pancakes

80 g/⅔ cup gluten-free plain/
all-purpose flour

2 eggs

1 teaspoon salt

butter, for frying

an ovenproof dish

Serves 3–4

To make the tomato sauce, heat the oil in a large saucepan, add the onion and garlic, season well with salt and pepper and cook for about 2–3 minutes.

Pour the tomatoes into a large bowl and squash them with your hands to break them into small pieces. Pour the tomatoes into the pan with the onions, taking care as the oil may spit as you pour them in, stir and leave to simmer for 2–2½ hours until the tomato sauce is thick and a deep rich colour. Leave to cool.

Next make the béchamel sauce. In a saucepan, melt the butter over a gentle heat, then add the cornflour/cornstarch and stir in well. Add the milk to the pan gradually, whisking all the time, then add the bay leaves. Cook for a few minutes until the sauce starts to thicken. Gradually add the cream and continue to stir over the heat until you have a smooth white sauce. Season with salt and pepper and set aside to cool. When cool, remove the bay leaves from the sauce.

For the filling, cook the spinach in salted boiling water for a few minutes, until the leaves just start to wilt but are still bright green. Strain, blanch in cold water, then strain again and firmly squeeze out all of the water. Finely chop the spinach with a sharp knife. Mix the spinach with the ricotta and season with salt and pepper, nutmeg and the lemon juice and zest, then fold in the Parmesan.

For the pancakes, whisk together the flour, eggs, salt and 200 ml/¾ cup water in a large mixing bowl until you have a thin batter. Heat a little butter in a frying pan, swirl it around to grease the pan, then pour off any excess butter. Add a ladleful of batter to the pan, swirling the pan as you pour the batter in to make sure that the whole base of the pan is coated in a thin layer. Once the batter is cooked through, turn the pancake over, either by flipping it (if you are brave!) or by using a spatula, and cook for a few minutes more on the other side. When cooked, transfer the pancake to a plate and repeat the process until all the batter is used, adding a little more butter to the pan each time, if necessary.

Preheat the oven to 180°C (350°F) Gas 4. Spoon a line of the ricotta mixture towards one end of a pancake, then roll it up. Repeat with the remaining pancakes until all the filling is used up. Spoon a few tablespoons of the tomato sauce into the baking dish and lay the pancakes in the dish. Spoon over more of the tomato sauce, then pour over the béchamel sauce. Sprinkle the top with a little grated Parmesan and black pepper and bake in the preheated oven for 20–25 minutes until the cheese turns golden brown. Serve straight away.

While traditionally a dessert, this chicken crumble is no less delicious and makes a satisfying meal. If you are short of time, you can use ready-cooked chicken and bought chicken stock.

chicken & mushroom crumble

Put the wine, carrot, leek, onion, bay leaves and peppercorns in a large saucepan and add the whole chicken. Fill the pan with cold water so that the chicken is covered. Bring the liquid to the boil, the reduce the heat and leave to simmer for an hour until the chicken is cooked through. Remove the chicken from the pan and strain the stock, discarding the vegetables. Store the stock in the refrigerator until needed to cook the spinach.

Once cold, remove the chicken skin, cut away the chicken meat from the bones and chop it into bite-sized pieces. Discard the bones and skin and keep the chicken in the refrigerator until needed.

Preheat the oven to 180°C (350°F) Gas 4.

Melt the butter in a large saucepan, then add the mushrooms and spring onions/scallions and cook for about 3–5 minutes until soft. Add the cornflour/cornstarch to the pan and stir well. Cook over the heat for a few minutes then add the cream and 200 ml/¾ cup of the reserved chicken stock. Season with salt and pepper and simmer until the sauce thickens. Add the mustard and chicken to the pan and stir well so that everything is coated, then pour the mixture into the ovenproof dish.

In another saucepan, heat the remaining chicken stock then add the spinach and cook for 2–3 minutes until the spinach just starts to wilt. Drain and discard the stock (or cool and freeze for another day) and distribute the spinach in small spoonfuls evenly throughout the chicken mixture.

For the crumble topping, put the oats, flour (plus baking powder and xanthan gum, if using) and cornmeal in a bowl and rub the butter in with your fingertips until the mixture comes together in large lumps. Season with salt and pepper. Sprinkle the crumble over the creamy chicken filling so that it is evenly distributed, then bake in the preheated oven for 25–30 minutes until the crumble topping is golden brown. Serve straight away.

For the filling

250 ml/1 cup white wine

1 large carrot, peeled and chopped

1 leek, trimmed and sliced

1 onion, halved

2 bay leaves

1 teaspoon peppercorns

1 medium chicken (about 1.2 kg/ 2 lb. 10 oz.)

50 g/3½ tablespoons butter

250 g/9 oz. chestnut/cremini mushrooms, quartered

3 spring onions/scallions, finely chopped

2 tablespoons cornflour/cornstarch

400 ml/1⅔ cups double/heavy cream

1 tablespoon wholegrain mustard

100 g/3½ oz. spinach

sea salt and ground black pepper

For the crumble topping

120 g/1 cup gluten-free rolled oats

80 g gluten-free self-raising flour OR ⅔ cup gluten-free all-purpose flour plus ¾ teaspoon baking powder and ½ teaspoon xanthan gum

40 g/⅓ cup fine cornmeal

100 g/6½ tablespoons butter, chilled

an ovenproof baking dish

Serves 4

This recipe was inspired by the wonderful chef Martin Lee at the Plough Restaurant in Bolnhurst, England. Gnudi are similar to gnocchi but are lighter as they are made without the potato. The gnudi can be prepared ahead of time and cooked shortly before serving. Baked with a light lemon sauce and Parmesan they are perfect served with a green salad.

gnudi bake

For the gnudi

500 g/1 lb. 2 oz. spinach

250 g/9 oz. ricotta

freshly squeezed juice and
    grated zest of 1 lemon

a pinch of nutmeg

fine cornmeal, for dusting

For the sauce

freshly squeezed juice of
    2 lemons

50 g/3½ tablespoons butter

3 tablespoons grated Parmesan
    cheese

sea salt and ground black pepper

an ovenproof dish

Serves 2

Cook the spinach in boiling salted water for a few minutes until it is just wilted but still has a vibrant green colour. Drain, then plunge into cold water. When the spinach is cold, drain the water again and put the spinach in a clean dish towel and squeeze tightly to remove all the water. You need the spinach to be really dry so that the Gnudi are not soggy, so take the time to remove as much water as possible. Using a sharp knife, chop the spinach very finely and set aside.

In a large mixing bowl, mix the chopped spinach with the ricotta. Season with the lemon zest and juice, nutmeg and salt and pepper and mix well. Take small pieces of the mixture and roll it into balls the size of a walnut in your hands. Dust each gnudi lightly in the cornmeal as you go and place on a baking sheet. Continue until all the mixture is used up – it will make about 16 gnudi. Leave the gnudi to chill in the refrigerator for at least an hour.

When you are ready to serve, preheat the oven to 180°C (350°F) Gas 4.

Bring a saucepan of salted water to the boil, then turn it down to a simmer. Poach the gnudi for about 2 minutes (it is best to do this in batches), then remove them from the water with a slotted spoon, drain and place in the baking dish.

In a saucepan, heat the lemon juice and butter and stir until they have emulsified and become shiny. Season with salt and pepper. Pour the sauce over the gnudi and sprinkle with the grated Parmesan. Bake in the preheated oven for 3–5 minutes until the cheese has just melted. Serve straight away.

Whilst sweet cheesecakes are one of the world's best-loved desserts, this unusual cheesecake is just as delicious. Packed with slow roasted tomatoes, fresh basil and crumbly feta cheese, this dish is a true slice of the Mediterranean. It is very rich, so you only need to serve small slices, accompanied by a dressed green salad.

sundried tomato & feta cheesecake

Preheat the oven to 180°C (350°F) Gas 4.

Put the tomatoes in a roasting pan, drizzle them with olive oil and sprinkle with the sugar, salt and pepper. Bake in the preheated oven for 20 minutes, then turn the temperature down to 140°C (275°F) Gas 1 and slow roast for a further hour. Remove from the oven and leave to cool in the pan.

Turn the oven up to 170°C (325°F) Gas 3.

Blitz the oatcakes to fine crumbs in a food processor or put them in a clean plastic bag and bash with a rolling pin. Transfer the crumbs to a large mixing bowl and stir in the melted butter. Tip the crumbs into the prepared cake pan and press them firmly into the base of the pan using the back of a spoon. Wrap the pan in clingfilm/plastic wrap and place in a large roasting pan half full of water, so that the water comes half way up the cheesecake pan.

For the filling, whisk together the crème fraîche, eggs, cream cheese and flour. Add half of the roasted tomatoes and their juices and oil from the pan to the cheese mixture, along with the chopped basil and the feta cheese. Fold in so that everything is evenly distributed and season with salt and pepper. Pour the mixture over the oatcake base.

Arrange the remaining tomatoes on top of the cheesecake, keeping some of them on the vine for decoration if you wish. Transfer the pan, in its water bath, to the preheated oven and bake for 1–1½ hours until golden brown on top and the cheesecake still has a slight wobble in the centre. Remove the cheesecake from the water and leave to cool, then transfer to the refrigerator to chill for at least 3 hours, or preferably overnight. The cheesecake will keep for up to 3 days in the refrigerator.

For the filling
600 g/1 lb. 5 oz. cherry vine tomatoes
olive oil, to drizzle
2 teaspoons caster/granulated sugar
600 ml/2½ cups crème fraîche
4 eggs
600 g/1 lb. 5 oz. cream cheese
2 tablespoons gluten-free plain/all-purpose flour, sifted
20 g/a large handful fresh basil, chopped
200 g/7 oz. feta cheese
sea salt and ground black pepper

For the base
250 g/9 oz. gluten-free oatcakes (see recipe on page 76 or store-bought)
125 g/1 stick butter, melted

a 25-cm/10-inch spring form cake pan, greased and lined with non-stick baking paper

Serves 12

A steamed suet pudding is real comfort food and gluten-free suet pastry
works really well as the suet prevents the pastry from being crumbly and dry.

steak & kidney pudding

For the filling

1 onion, finely sliced

1–2 tablespoons olive oil

450 g/1 lb. stewing beef, diced

50 g/2 oz. ox kidneys, chopped

150 ml/⅔ cup medium sweet
   sherry

120 ml/½ cup beef stock

100 g/3½ oz. baby carrots,
   trimmed

3 open cap mushrooms, quartered

1 tablespoon cornflour/cornstarch

sea salt and ground black pepper

For the suet crust

225 g gluten-free self-raising flour
   plus 1 teaspoon baking powder
   OR 1¾ cups gluten-free all-
   purpose flour plus 3 teaspoons
   baking powder and
   1½ teaspoons xanthan gum,
   plus extra flour for dusting

100 g gluten-free shredded suet
   OR 6½ tablespoons vegetable
   shortening, chilled and grated
   (see page 11)

2 teaspoons gluten-free Dijon
   mustard

½ teaspoon salt

about 240 ml/1 cup milk

a large flameproof lidded casserole

*a 900-ml/3½-cup pudding basin,
greased*

kitchen string

Serves 4

Preheat the oven to 180°C (350°F) Gas 4.

Put the onion in the casserole with the olive oil, season and cook over a gentle heat, until it starts to turn lightly golden. Remove from the pan and set aside. Add the beef to the pan with a little further oil and cook until it is lightly browned on the outside to seal it. Add the kidneys to the pan and cook for 2–3 minutes, stirring all the time. Add the sherry and cook for a few minutes, then add the cooked onion, stock, carrots and mushrooms, and season to taste.

Put the lid on the casserole, transfer it to the preheated oven and cook for 1 hour, turning the temperature down to 170°C (325°F) Gas 3 after 30 minutes. Remove a few spoonfuls of the juices from the pan, mix well with the cornflour/cornstarch, then stir back into the meat to thicken the sauce, then leave to cool.

For the pastry, put the flour, baking powder (plus xanthan gum, if using), suet/vegetable shortening, mustard and salt in a large mixing bowl and gradually add the milk (you may not need it all) until you have a smooth dough that is not sticky.

On a flour-dusted surface, roll out the pastry to a circle measuring about 26 cm/10 inches in diameter and about 8 mm/⅜ inch thick. Cut away a quarter of the dough circle and set aside. Wet the inside edges of the dough where the quarter has been cut away with a little water and use the dough to line the pudding basin. Due to the shape of the basin, the two cut away edges of the dough should meet, so press them together. On a flour-dusted surface, roll the remaining quarter of dough out into a circle the size of the top of the pudding basin. Spoon the cooled meat mixture into the pudding basin. Wet the edges of the top of the pastry in the basin with a little water, then place the dough circle on top and press down with your fingers to seal.

Fold a sheet of non-stick baking paper in half. Make a pleat in the centre and place it over the pudding basin (the pleat will allow for the pastry rising as it cooks). Press the paper over the edges of the basin and tie around the top with string. Cover with kitchen foil and tie extra string around the basin and over the top to make a handle to lift the basin in and out of the pan with.

Set a trivet in the bottom of a large lidded saucepan and half fill with water. Lower the basin into the pan, so that the water comes half way up the basin (not too high or water may get into the pudding). Put the lid on the pan and steam the pudding on the hob/stovetop for 3 hours. Once cooked, use the string handle to lift the basin out of the pan. Leave to cool for a few minutes, then remove the foil and baking paper. Slide a knife around the edge of the pudding between the pastry and the basin to loosen it. Place a serving plate on top of the pudding basin and, using oven mitts or a towel to protect your hands, carefully invert the basin onto the plate. Remove the basin to reveal the pudding and serve straight away.

Tarte Flambée was one of the things I always ate when we went on family holidays to the Alsace region in France. Topped with bacon, goats' cheese and honey, it is the perfect sweet and salty combination. Truffle honey is delicious on this slice, but if you do not have any, substitute with runny honey and a drizzle of truffle oil instead.

tarte flambée

Put the warm milk, yeast and sugar in a jug/pitcher and leave for about 10 minutes until the yeast has activated and a foam has formed on top of the liquid.

Put the flour in a large mixing bowl and mix in the egg, yeast mixture, salt and 60 ml/¼ cup of the olive oil with your hands until you have a smooth soft dough. Form the dough into a ball, then add the remaining olive oil to the bowl and roll the dough in the oil until it is absorbed.

Transfer the dough to the prepared baking sheet and press it out very thinly into a large rectangle approximately 40 cm x 25 cm/16 x 10 inches using your fingertips or a rolling pin. Leave the dough in a warm place to prove for about an hour until the dough becomes puffy.

Preheat the oven to 180°C (350°F) Gas 4.

Cook the bacon in a dry frying pan until golden brown. Slice the onion very finely (this is best done on a mandolin if you have one). Add the onion to the pan with the bacon and cook for a few minutes until softened, then leave to cool.

Spoon the crème fraîche over the base of the dough and spread it out thinly. Sprinkle over the bacon and onion. Cut the goats' cheese into thin slices and distribute evenly over the top of the dough. Drizzle the tart with a little of the honey and bake in the preheated oven for 20–25 minutes until the dough is crisp and the cheese is melted and golden brown. Serve straight away drizzled with a little extra honey, if you wish.

For the tart base

100 ml/6½ tablespoons warm milk

1 tablespoon fast-action dried yeast

1 tablespoon caster/granulated sugar

250 g/2 cups gluten-free strong white bread flour, sifted

1 egg

½ teaspoon salt

80 ml/⅓ cup olive oil

For the topping

250 g bacon lardons/1⅓ cups thick-sliced back bacon, cut into cubes

1 small onion, peeled

250 ml/1 cup crème fraîche or sour cream

150 g/5½ oz. creamy goats' cheese

truffle honey, to drizzle

a large baking sheet, greased with olive oil

a mandolin (optional)

Serves 4

Making gluten-free toad-in-the-hole batter in the same way as a traditional batter does not work well and tends to result in a flat (rather than light and airy) pancake. However, a choux pastry dough makes a fantastic toad in the hole and you really won't know that it is gluten free.

toad in the hole

For the batter

65 g/½ cup gluten-free plain/
  all-purpose flour
50 g/3½ tablespoons butter
2 large eggs, beaten

For the toad

2 gluten-free sausages
1 small dessert apple
1 small onion
60–80 ml/¼–⅓ cup olive oil
sea salt and ground black pepper

a 4-hole Yorkshire pudding pan

a piping bag fitted with a large nozzle/tip

Serves 2

Preheat the oven to 180°C (350°F) Gas 4.

Twist each sausage in half tightly to make 4 mini sausages. Cut the apple into quarters and remove the core leaving the skins on, then cut each quarter into 3 slices. Peel the onion and cut into small wedges. Put the sausages, apple slices and onion in a roasting pan and drizzle with a little olive oil. Season, then roast in the oven for about 20 minutes until the sausages brown. Remove from the oven, then turn the oven temperature up to 200°C (400°F) Gas 6.

For the batter, sift the flour twice to remove any lumps. Heat the butter in a saucepan with 150 ml/⅔ cup water until the butter is melted, then bring to the boil. Add all of the flour quickly and remove the pan from the heat. Beat hard with a wooden spoon until the dough forms a ball and no longer sticks to the sides of the pan. Leave to cool for about 5 minutes. Whisk the beaten eggs into the flour mixture, a small amount at a time, using a balloon whisk. The mixture will form a sticky paste which holds its shape when you lift the whisk up.

Pour a large spoonful of oil into each hole of the pan, then put it in the oven for 5 minutes until the oil gets very hot. Meanwhile, spoon the batter into the piping bag. Pipe a large ring of dough into the hot oil in each hole of the pan. Place a sausage and some apple and onion slices into the centre of each hole and return to the oven for 25–30 minutes until the batter has risen and is crisp and golden brown. Serve straight away.

This delicious spiced cake is great to serve with dhal or can be eaten on its own as an Indian snack.

Tanuja's Indian spiced cake

For the spiced cake, mix the ondhwa flour, cornmeal and bicarbonate of soda/baking soda together in a large mixing bowl and stir in the yogurt, corn oil and 375 ml/1½ cups of cold water. Stir well so that everything is thoroughly combined, then leave to stand while you prepare the vegetables.

In a large frying pan, heat the tablespoon of ghee for the cake and fry the onion and chilli until soft. Add the salt, grated courgette/zucchini and carrot, and green beans and cook until the vegetables are soft. Add the peas to the pan along with the curry powder, garam masala, cumin seeds and turmeric and cook for a few minutes until you can smell a strong aroma of the spices. Stir in the coriander/cilantro and lime pickle, then remove from the heat and leave to cool slightly. Spoon the spiced vegetables into the flour and yogurt mixture.

Preheat the oven to 180°C (350°F) Gas 4.

In a second frying pan, heat the ghee for the spiced ghee and, once melted, add the cloves, cinnamon, black onion seeds and curry leaves and cook for a few minutes until the seeds start to pop. Pour the melted spiced ghee into the prepared cake pan, removing the cloves and cinnamon stick. Put the pan in the oven to heat the ghee. Once the ghee is hot, remove the pan from the oven and spoon the cake batter into the hot ghee. Sprinkle the top of the cake with the sesame seeds. Return to the oven and cook for about 30–40 minutes until the cake is golden brown and springs back to your touch.

For the dhal, put the red lentils and chopped onion in a large heavy based saucepan with 1 litre/4 cups of water and set over a gentle heat. Add the garam masala, turmeric, chillies, tomatoes, fenugreek and ginger and simmer for about 30–45 minutes until the lentils are soft and have absorbed some of the water. Add the coconut milk, season with salt and pepper and cook for a further 30 minutes until the lentils have thickened to a soup like texture.

Prepare the tarka by melting the ghee in a frying pan. Add the onion seeds, garlic and curry leaves and cook for a few minutes until the garlic is lightly golden and the onion seeds start to pop. Pour the tarka into the pan with the lentils all in one go – the dhal will sizzle as you do this – and cook the dhal for 5 minutes further. Serve straight away with the cake or leave to cool and then reheat to serve. The dhal will keep for up to 3 days in the refrigerator or can be frozen.

For the spiced cake
450 g/3 cups ondhwa flour
140 g/1 cup fine cornmeal
1 teaspoon bicarbonate of soda/baking soda
425 g/1 cups plain yogurt
250 ml/1 cup corn oil
1 generous tablespoon ghee (clarified butter)
1 red onion, finely sliced
1 red chilli, finely chopped
1 teaspoon salt
1 courgette/zucchini, grated
1 carrot, peeled and grated
150 g/5½ oz. green beans, finely chopped
150 g/1 cup frozen peas
1 tablespoon hot curry powder
1 tablespoon garam masala
1 teaspoon cumin seeds
1 teaspoon ground turmeric
a small bunch of fresh coriander/cilantro finely chopped
1 tablespoon lime pickle

For the spiced ghee
2 generous tablespoons ghee
10 cloves
1 cinnamon stick
1 tablespoon black onion seeds
1 tablespoon curry leaves
1 tablespoon sesame seeds

For the dhal
250 g/1⅔ cups split red lentils
½ onion, finely chopped
1 tablespoon garam masala
1 generous teaspoon ground turmeric
2 red chillies, whole
a 400-g/14-oz. can chopped tomatoes
1 teaspoon fenugreek
a 2.5-cm/1-inch piece of ginger, finely sliced
400 ml/1⅔ cups coconut milk
sea salt and ground black pepper

For the tarka
2 tablespoons ghee
1 tablespoon black onion seeds
2 garlic cloves, finely sliced
1 tablespoon curry leaves

a 30 x 20-cm/12 x 8-inch cake pan, greased and lined with non-stick baking paper

Serves 6

index

acknowledgments

A huge thanks, as always, to Ryland Peters and Small for allowing me to write a sequel gluten-free baking book – in particular, to my lovely friend Julia Charles for commissioning the book, Rebecca Woods for her brilliant editing, and Iona Hoyle for the beautiful design. To Bridget Sargeson and Jack Sargeson for the beautiful food styling and to William Reavell for producing stunning pictures – thank you all so much! Thanks, too, to my agent Heather Holden-Brown for her endless support. Particular thanks also to Lucy Deakin, my inspiration for this book, and to my wonderful friends and family for always being there.